LIGUORI CATHOLIC BIBLE STUDY

Prophets II

EZEKIEL AND DANIEL

WILLIAM A. ANDERSON, DMIN, PHD

Liguori
LIGUORI, MISSOURI

Imprimi Potest:
Harry Grile, CSsR, Provincial
Denver Province, The Redemptorists

Printed with Ecclesiastical Permission and Approved for Private or Instructional Use

Nihil Obstat: Rev. Msgr. Kevin Michael Quirk, JCD, JV
        Censor Librorum

Imprimatur: + Michael J. Bransfield
        Bishop of Wheeling-Charleston [West Virginia]
        November 26, 2013

Published by Liguori Publications
Liguori, Missouri 63057

To order, call 800-325-9521
www.liguori.org

Copyright © 2014 William A. Anderson

Cataloging-in-Publication Data is on file with the Library of Congress.

p ISBN 978-0-7648-2136-3
e ISBN 978-0-7648-6923-5

Liguori Publications, a nonprofit corporation, is an apostolate of The Redemptorists. To learn more about The Redemptorists, visit Redemptorists.com.

Printed in the United States of America
18 17 16 15 14 / 5 4 3 2 1
First Edition

Contents

NOTE: The length of each Bible section varies. Group leaders should combine sections as needed to fit the number of sessions in their program.

Dedication

THIS SERIES is lovingly dedicated to the memory of my parents, Angor and Kathleen Anderson, in gratitude for all they shared with all who knew them, especially my siblings and me.

Acknowledgments

BIBLE STUDIES and reflections depend on the help of others who read the manuscript and make suggestions. I am especially indebted to Sister Anne Francis Bartus, CSJ, DMin, whose vast experience and knowledge were very helpful in bringing this series to its final form.

About the Author

William A. Anderson, DMin, PhD, is a presbyter of the Diocese of Wheeling-Charleston, West Virginia. A director of retreats and parish missions, professor, catechist, spiritual director, and a former pastor, he has written extensively on pastoral, spiritual, and religious subjects. Father Anderson earned his doctor of ministry degree from St. Mary's Seminary & University in Baltimore, and his doctorate in sacred theology from Duquesne University in Pittsburgh.

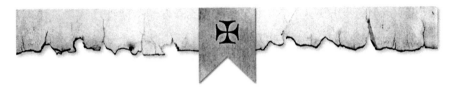

Introduction to
Liguori Catholic Bible Study

READING THE BIBLE can be daunting. It's a complex book, and many a person of goodwill has tried to read the Bible and ended up putting it down in utter confusion. It helps to have a companion, and *Liguori Catholic Bible Study* is a solid one. Over the course of this series, you'll learn about biblical messages, themes, personalities, and events and understand how the books of the Bible rose out of the need to address new situations.

Across the centuries, people of faith have asked, "Where is God in this moment?" Millions of Catholics look to the Bible for encouragement in their journey of faith. Wisdom teaches us not to undertake Bible study alone, disconnected from the Church that was given Scripture to share and treasure. When used as a source of prayer and thoughtful reflection, the Bible comes alive.

Your choice of a Bible-study program should be dictated by what you want to get out of it. One goal of *Liguori Catholic Bible Study* is to give readers greater familiarity with the Bible's structure, themes, personalities, and message. But that's not enough. This program will also teach you to use Scripture in your prayer. God's message is as compelling and urgent today as ever, but we get only part of the message when it's memorized and stuck in our head. It's meant for the entire person—physical, emotional, and spiritual.

We're baptized into life with Christ, and we're called to live more fully with Christ today as we practice the values of justice, peace, forgiveness, and community. God's new covenant was written on the hearts of the people of Israel; we, their spiritual descendants, are loved that intimately by God today. *Liguori Catholic Bible Study* will draw you closer to God, in whose image and likeness we are fashioned.

Group and Individual Study

The *Liguori Catholic Bible Study* series is intended for group and individual study and prayer. This series gives you the tools to start a study group. Gathering two or three people in a home or announcing the meeting of a Bible-study group in a parish or community can bring surprising results. Each lesson in this series contains a section to help groups study, reflect, pray, and share biblical reflections. Each lesson but the first also has a second section for individual study.

Many people who want to learn more about the Bible don't know where to begin. This series gives them a place to start and helps them continue until they're familiar with all the books of the Bible.

Bible study can be a lifelong project, always enriching those who wish to be faithful to God's Word. When people complete a study of the whole Bible, they can begin again, making new discoveries with each new adventure into the Word of God.

Lectio Divina
(Sacred Reading)

BIBLE STUDY isn't just a matter of gaining intellectual knowledge of the Bible; it's also about gaining a greater understanding of God's love and concern for creation. The purpose of reading and knowing the Bible is to enrich our relationship with God. God loves us and gave us the Bible to illustrate that love. In his April 12, 2013, address before the Pontifical Biblical Commission, Pope Francis stressed that "the Church's life and mission are founded on the word of God, which is the soul of theology and at the same time inspires the whole of Christian life."

The Meaning of *Lectio Divina*

Lectio divina is a Latin expression that means "divine or sacred reading." The process for *lectio divina* consists of Scripture readings, reflection, and prayer. Many clergy, religious, and laity use *lectio divina* in their daily spiritual reading to develop a closer and more loving relationship with God. Learning about Scripture has as its purpose the living of its message, which demands a period of reflection on Scripture passages.

Prayer and *Lectio Divina*

Prayer is a necessary element for the practice of *lectio divina*. The entire process of reading and reflecting is a prayer. It's not merely an intellectual pursuit; it's also a spiritual one. Page 15 includes an opening prayer for gathering one's thoughts before moving on to the passages in each section. This prayer may be used privately or in a group. For those who use the book for daily spiritual reading, the prayer for each section may be repeated each day. Some may wish to keep a journal of each day's meditation.

Pondering the Word of God

Lectio divina is the ancient Christian spiritual practice of reading the holy Scriptures with intentionality and devotion. This practice helps Christians center themselves and descend to the level of the heart to enter an inner quiet space, finding God.

This sacred reading is distinct from reading for knowledge or information, and it's more than the pious practice of spiritual reading. It is the practice of opening ourselves to the action and inspiration of the Holy Spirit. As we intentionally focus on and become present to the inner meaning of the Scripture passage, the Holy Spirit enlightens our minds and hearts. We come to the text willing to be influenced by a deeper meaning that lies within the words and thoughts we ponder.

In this space, we open ourselves to be challenged and changed by the inner meaning we experience. We approach the text in a spirit of faith and obedience as a disciple ready to be taught by the Holy Spirit. As we savor the sacred text, we let go of our usual control of how we expect God to act in our lives and surrender our heart and conscience to the flow of the divine (*divina*) through the reading (*lectio*).

The fundamental principle of *lectio divina* leads us to understand the profound mystery of the Incarnation, "The Word became flesh," not only in history but also within us.

Praying *Lectio* Today

Before you begin, relax your body and maintain a posture of prayer (back straight, eyes shut, feet flat on the floor). Then practice these four simple actions:

1. Read a passage from Scripture or the daily Mass readings. This is known as *lectio*. (If the Word of God is read aloud, the hearers listen attentively.)

2. Pray the selected passage with attention as you listen for a specific meaning that comes to mind. Once again, the reading is listened to or silently read and reflected or meditated on. This is known as *meditatio*.

3. The exercise becomes active. Pick a word, sentence, or idea that surfaces from your consideration of the chosen text. Does the reading remind you of a person, place, or experience? If so, pray about it. Compose your thoughts and reflection into a simple word or phrase. This prayer-thought will help you remove distractions during the *lectio*. This exercise is called *oratio*.

4. In silence, with your eyes closed, quiet yourself and become conscious of your breathing. Let your thoughts, feelings, and concerns fade as you consider the selected passage in the previous step (*oratio*). If you're distracted, use your prayer word to help you return to silence. This is *contemplatio*.

This exercise can take as long as you want, but in the context of this Bible study, 10 to 20 minutes should be sufficient.

Many teachers of prayer call contemplation the prayer of resting in God, a prelude to losing oneself in the presence of God. Scripture is transformed in our hearing as we pray and allow our hearts to unite intimately with the Lord. The Word truly takes on flesh, and this time it is manifested in our flesh.

How to Use This
Bible-Study Companion

THE BIBLE, along with the commentaries and reflections found in this study, will help participants become familiar with the Scripture texts and lead them to reflect more deeply on the texts' messages. At the end of this study, participants will have a firm grasp of the Books of Ezekiel and Daniel, becoming therefore more cognizant of the spiritual nourishment these books offer. This study is not only an intellectual adventure, it's also a spiritual one. The reflections lead participants into their own journey with the Scripture readings.

Context

When the authors wrote and edited the Books of Ezekiel and Daniel, they were dealing with a people living in captivity and persecution under foreign kings. To help readers learn about each passage in relation to those around it, each lesson begins with an overview that puts the Scripture passages into context.

Part 1: Group Study

To give participants a comprehensive study of the Books of Ezekiel and Daniel, the present text is divided into seven lessons. Lesson 1 is group study only; Lessons 2 through 7 are divided into Part 1, group study, and Part 2, individual study. For example, Lesson 2 covers passages from Ezekiel 4—15. The study group reads and discusses chapters 4—7 (Part 1). Participants privately read and reflect on Ezekiel 8—15 (Part 2).

Group study may or may not include *lectio divina*. With *lectio divina*, the group meets for ninety minutes using the first format on page 13. Without *lectio divina*, the group meets for one hour using the format at the bottom of page 13, and participants are urged to privately read the *lectio divina* section at the end of Part 1. It contains additional reflections on the Scripture passages studied during the group session that will take participants even further into the passages.

Part 2: Individual Study

The passages not covered in Part 1 are divided into shorter components, one to be studied each day. Participants who don't belong to a study group can use the lessons for private sacred reading. They may choose to reflect on one Scripture passage per day, making it possible for a clearer understanding of the Scripture passages used in their *lectio divina* (sacred reading).

A PROCESS FOR SACRED READING

Liguori Publications has designed this study to be user-friendly and manageable. However, group dynamics and leaders vary. We're not trying to keep the Holy Spirit from working in your midst, thus we suggest you decide beforehand which format works best for your group. If you have limited time, you could study the Bible as a group and save prayer and reflection for personal time.

However, if your group wishes to digest and feast on sacred Scripture through both prayer and study, we recommend you spend closer to ninety minutes each week by gathering to study and pray with Scripture. *Lectio divina* (see page 8) is an ancient contemplative prayer form that moves readers from the head to the heart in meeting the Lord. We strongly suggest using this prayer form whether in individual or group study.

GROUP-STUDY FORMATS

1. Bible Study With *Lectio Divina*

About ninety minutes of group study

- ✠ Gathering and opening prayer (3–5 minutes)
- ✠ Read Scripture passage aloud (5 minutes)
- ✠ Silently review the commentary and prepare to discuss it with the group (3–5 minutes)
- ✠ Discuss the Scripture passage along with the commentary and reflection (30 minutes)
- ✠ Read each Scripture passage aloud a second time, followed by quiet time for meditation and contemplation (5 minutes)
- ✠ Spend some time in prayer with the selected passage. Group participants will slowly read the Scripture passage a third time in silence, listening for the voice of God as they read (10–20 minutes)
- ✠ Shared reflection (10–15 minutes)
- ✠ Closing prayer (3–5 minutes)

To become acquainted with lectio divina, *see page 8.*

2. Bible Study

About one hour of group study

- ✠ Gathering and opening prayer (3–5 minutes)
- ✠ Read each Scripture passage aloud (5 minutes)
- ✠ Silently review the commentary and prepare to discuss it with the group (3–5 minutes)
- ✠ Discuss the Scripture passage along with the commentary and reflections (40 minutes)
- ✠ Closing prayer (3–5 minutes)

Notes to the Leader

- ✠ Bring a copy of the *New American Bible,* revised edition.
- ✠ Plan which sections will be covered each week of your Bible study.
- ✠ Read the material in advance of each session.
- ✠ Establish written ground rules. (Example: We won't keep you longer than ninety minutes; don't dominate the sharing by arguing or debating.)
- ✠ Meet in an appropriate and welcoming gathering space (church building, meeting room, house).
- ✠ Provide name tags and perhaps use a brief icebreaker for the first meeting; ask participants to introduce themselves.
- ✠ Mark the Scripture passage(s) that will be read during the session.
- ✠ Decide how you would like the Scripture to be read aloud (whether by one or multiple readers).
- ✠ Use a clock or watch.
- ✠ Provide extra Bibles (or copies of the Scripture passages) for participants who don't bring their Bible.
- ✠ Ask participants to read "Introduction: Prophets II" (page 16) before the first session.
- ✠ Tell participants which passages to study and urge them to read the passages and commentaries before the meeting.
- ✠ If you opt to use the *lectio divina* format, familiarize yourself with this prayer form ahead of time.

Notes to the Participants

- ✠ Bring a copy of the *New American Bible,* revised edition.
- ✠ Read "Introduction: Prophets II" (page 16) before the first session.
- ✠ Read the Scripture passages and commentaries before each session.
- ✠ Be prepared to share and listen respectfully. (This is not a time to debate beliefs or argue.)

Opening Prayer

Leader: O God, come to my assistance.

Response: O Lord, make haste to help me.

Leader: Glory be to the Father, and to the Son, and to the Holy Spirit...

Response: ...as it was in the beginning, is now, and ever shall be, world without end. Amen.

Leader: Christ is the vine and we are the branches. As branches linked to Jesus, the vine, we are called to recognize that the Scriptures are always being fulfilled in our lives. It is the living Word of God living on in us. Come, Holy Spirit, fill the hearts of your faithful and kindle in us the fire of your divine wisdom, knowledge, and love.

Response: Open our minds and hearts as we study your great love for us as shown in the Bible.

Reader: (Open your Bible to the assigned Scripture(s) and read in a paced, deliberate manner. Pause for one minute, listening for a word, phrase, or image that you may use in your *lectio divina* practice.)

Closing Prayer

Leader: Let us pray as Jesus taught us.

Response: Our Father...

Leader: Lord, inspire us with your Spirit as we study your Word in the Bible. Be with us this day and every day as we strive to know you and serve you and to love as you love. We believe that through your goodness and love, the Spirit of the Lord is truly upon us. Allow the words of the Bible, your Word, to capture us and inspire us to live as you live and to love as you love.

Response: Amen.

Leader: May the divine assistance remain with us always.

Response: In the name of the Father, and of the Son, and of the Holy Spirit. Amen.

Prophets II

EZEKIEL AND DANIEL

Read this overview before the first lesson.

THE ROLE OF THE PROPHETS was to communicate God's message to the people and to communicate with the Lord on behalf of the people. Prophets did not receive their office through heredity as did the priests of the Old Testament, but they received their call from God, often through an intermediary sent by God. Since they were chosen by the Lord, prophets often began their message with "Thus says the LORD," or something similar. Unlike the priesthood of the Old Testament, which was limited to males, prophets could be male or female. In the Book of Judges, a woman named Deborah is identified as a prophet (see Judges 4:4).

Although we refer to the prophetic writings as "books," they are often a composite of prophetic messages written or spoken by the prophet over time. Often, the followers of the prophets would hear the prophet's spoken message and later put it in writing. The writings of the prophets also could have been revealed at one time and, when the historical climate changed, committed to writing or editing at a later time. Throughout history, some prophetic writings were edited several times before they reached their final form.

Although many people think of prophets as predicting the future, prophets mainly addressed the current issues of their era. At times they did predict the future, often as a warning about some destruction that was to afflict the people if they did not turn their hearts back to the Lord. Many of the prophets predicted a time of peace and redemption for the Israelites after a long period of affliction. They were not always popular figures among their own people. Totally dedicated to the Lord and the covenant, true prophets courageously conveyed the Word of the Lord to the people, despite the rejection, persecution, and death they had to endure.

This volume of *Liguori Catholic Bible Series* will study the Books of Ezekiel and Daniel.

Historical Perspective

The history of the prophets of Israel consists of several major periods that influenced the manner of writing and the interpretations given to the writing by later editors.

(1) The first period includes the era of the kings in Israel and Judah, from the eleventh to the ninth century before Christ.

(2) The second period includes the era of Assyrian domination which took place in the eighth century when Assyria conquered and destroyed the northern kingdom of Israel in 721 BC, scattering many of its captive inhabitants among other nations.

(3) The third period includes the Babylonian crisis that took place from the seventh century to the early part of the sixth century before Christ, when Babylon invaded Judah and forced many of its inhabitants into exile in Babylon. Many others fled for refuge in foreign lands.

(4) The fourth period includes the era from the late sixth to the middle of the fifth century before Christ when Cyrus of Persia conquered the Babylonians and allowed the Israelites to return home to Judah.

(5) In the Book of Daniel, the reader encounters a period of confusion and oppression for the Israelites which took place from the fourth to the second century. Alexander the Great conquered the Persians and by 333 BC he had established a powerful Greek Empire. Since Jerusalem and Judea (a new name for Judah) were part of the Persian Empire, they now belonged to the Greek Empire. Alexander allowed the Jews to practice their faith as they wished. He died in 323 BC at age thirty-two, and his kingdom split into at least four parts, each one ruled by one of Alexander's generals.

Shortly after Alexander's death, one general, Ptolemy, took over Egypt and Jerusalem, and Ptolomaic rule lasted for the next 120 years. Like Alexander, he allowed the people of Judea to follow their own God and ways. In 198 BC, King Antiochus III, the Seleucid, conquered Israel and Jerusalem and allowed the Jews to continue their religious practices with their own high priest. After losing a battle to the Romans, King Antiochus III was in dire need of finances. In an attempt to raid a Babylonian temple for plunder, King Antiochus III was killed. His successor, who ruled for twelve years, fruitlessly attempted to loot the Temple in Jerusalem. After the death of Antiochus III's successor, Antiochus IV usurped the kingship.

Antiochus IV fought against the Ptolemy power in Egypt. Returning from Egypt after a victory over the Ptolemies in Egypt, Antiochus IV, still in need of funds, raided Jerusalem and ransacked all the gold from the Temple. Years later, in response to a rebellion against a high priest appointed by Antiochus IV, Antiochus unleashed a horrifying persecution of the Jews. This appears to be the era in which the author of Daniel was writing the second part of his book (165–163 BC) from chapter 7 to 13, with many apocalyptic allusions to the turmoil endured under the Seleucid king.

In Judea, two factions existed among the Jews since the time of Alexander, the traditionalist faction consisting of Jews who clung desperately to their God and Jewish traditions, and the Hellenized faction favoring the Greek culture, language, and gods. Antiochus sided with the Hellenized Jews and erected a statue of Zeus in the Jewish Temple, ordering the Jews to accept Greek culture and worship Zeus. The faithful Jews considered the erection of the statue of Zeus in the Temple an abomination and rebelled against the king.

The Book of Ezekiel (I)

EZEKIEL 1–3

Their children [the Israelites] are bold of face and stubborn of heart—to them I am sending you. You shall say to them: Thus says the LORD GOD. And whether they hear or resist—they are a rebellious house—they shall know that a prophet has been among them (2:4–5).

Opening Prayer (SEE PAGE 15)

Context

Ezekiel 1—3 The Book of Ezekiel opens with Ezekiel's visions of the glory of the Lord, his call to be a prophet, the duties of a prophet, and the limits of Ezekiel's prophetic ministry. Ezekiel, who is in exile in Babylon, received a vision of four living creatures with human forms, large wings, and four faces resembling the faces of animals with wheels alongside each of the creatures. Above them was something looking like "the firmament." Above the firmament was a likeness of a throne. A voice told Ezekiel he will be sent to the Israelites as a sentinel, which means he will be sent as a prophet to the house of Israel. A hand stretched out and gave Ezekiel a scroll to eat. The Lord struck Ezekiel mute, so he can only speak when he is speaking the Word of the Lord.

GROUP STUDY (EZEKIEL 1—3)

Read aloud Ezekiel 1—3.

1 Ezekiel's First Vision

The opening sentences of the book identify Ezekiel and the time of his visions. Since he was born into a priestly family around the year 623 BC, he was a priest with a deep concern for the Temple in Jerusalem. An accounting of the dates found in the Book of Ezekiel implies he was sent into exile in Babylon at the age of twenty-five, received his call as a prophet at the age of thirty, and received his last vision at the age of fifty-two.

Long before the birth of Ezekiel, Judah had become a vassal of the powerful nation of Assyria, but the Assyrian Empire rapidly declined after 630 BC, eventually being replaced by the mighty army of the Babylonian Empire. Around 609 BC, Judah became a vassal of the Babylonians (Chaldeans). In time, the king of Judah, tired of paying tribute to Babylon, incited an unsuccessful rebellion against Nebuchadnezzar, the king of Babylon, which led to a defeat at the hands of the Babylonians in 597 BC and the deportation of thousands of the leading people of Judah, including King Jehoiachin of Judah and Ezekiel the priest.

Ten years later (587 BC), a second deportation took place when the Israelites again failed in an attempt to rebel against the Babylonians. As a result of the rebellion, Babylon angrily ravaged all of Judah, including Jerusalem, destroying the Temple, killing thousands of Israelites, and leading the majority of the inhabitants into exile.

On the fifth day of the fourth month—July 31, 593 BC—Ezekiel, while in exile, received his initial vision from the Lord. This vision took place in the thirtieth year. Commentators believe the number referred to the age of Ezekiel, which would be logical, since the thirtieth year was the year those born into the priestly family would begin to serve as a priest for the nation. The Word of the Lord came to Ezekiel in the land of the Chaldeans (Babylonians) by the river Chebar, which was one of the canals of the Euphrates River, where a colony of Jews lived.

Ezekiel attempts to explain his heavenly vision, presenting it in a highly symbolic and vague manner. He perceives a strong wind coming from the north. For the people of Ezekiel's day, the north was the usual dwelling of the gods. In the vision, he witnesses a large cloud, flashing with fire, glowing, with something like polished metal gleaming at its center. From within the cloud appear figures looking like four living creatures, each with a human form. Later, in Ezekiel 10:1, Ezekiel will identify these living creatures as cherubim. Cherubim are often depicted with the bodies of bulls or lions, with wings like those of an eagle, and a human head.

In Ezekiel's vision, the living creatures have four faces, four wings, straight legs, and hooves like those of a bull. He perceives human hands under their wings, and the wings of one touched the wings of another. They move straight ahead. Their faces, which seemed to express some virtue or strength, look in four different directions. One face was that of a human being (intelligence), next to it on the right the face of a lion (wild animals), on the left was the face of an ox (powerful livestock), and the face of an eagle facing backward (swift and powerful birds). The faces looking in four directions symbolize that the Lord sees all.

The living creatures move straight ahead, with an appearance like burning coals darting back and forth among the creatures, with flashes of lightening. In chapter 10, Ezekiel will identify the brightness of the living creatures as the glory of the Lord. Some commentators compare the strange scene in Ezekiel's vision to that of a giant chariot that carries the glory of the Lord.

Alongside each of the living creatures, Ezekiel sees yellow, sparkling wheels, similar to each other and appearing as though one wheel is inside the other. They move in the direction the living creatures moved, straight ahead and rising from the ground with the living creatures when they rose up, and remaining stationary when the living creatures remained stationary. Eyes filled the rim of the wheels all around, symbolizing that the Lord knows and sees all.

Ezekiel witnesses the firmament like a shining dome of crystal over the heads of the living creatures. The dome recalls the second day of creation when the Lord placed a dome over the earth to separate the water above the dome from the water below the dome (see Genesis 1:6–8). The living creatures reach out to each other, and the sound of the wings thunders like the voice of God. When they lower their wings, a voice comes from the firmament above their heads.

Above the firmament, Ezekiel sees a likeness of a throne with a figure that looks like a human being, appearing to look like fire from the waist up and fire and brilliance like a rainbow from the waist down. Ezekiel recognizes the vision as the glory of the Lord, and he falls on his face and hears a voice speak. As mentioned previously, the people of ancient times pictured the world as covered with a dome which kept the waters above (the sky was blue like water) from the waters below the dome. The Lord sits enthroned above this dome over the still waters. In the Book of Exodus, Moses and those with him saw the God of Israel enthroned, and under the Lord's feet appeared to be sapphire tile work, as clear as the sky (see Exodus 24:10). Ezekiel is about to learn of his mission.

2—3:4 Eating the Scroll

A voice in 2:1 addresses Ezekiel as "Son of man," a title referring to Ezekiel as belonging to the category of humanity, that is, as a human being. "Son of man" occurs ninety-three times in Ezekiel. The spirit of the Lord enters Ezekiel and empowers him to hear the Lord's Word. A second time, the voice uses the term "Son of man" when Ezekiel is sent to the Israelites. The use of the term indicates Ezekiel, God's messenger, is not an angel as found in other sections of the Bible, but a human being. Ezekiel's mission is to go to the Israelites who joined in the sin of their ancestors by rebelling against the Lord.

As the Lord's prophet, Ezekiel is to introduce his prophecies as did other prophets, with the words, "Thus says the LORD GOD." By this pronouncement, whether the Israelites accept his message or not, they will know that a prophet is in their midst. The voice of the Lord instructs Ezekiel not to fear this rebellious people or their words, even if they threaten him with briars, thorns, or sitting among scorpions. Ezekiel is to hear the Word of the Lord and not rebel like the Israelites do.

The Lord directs Ezekiel to open his mouth and eat what the Lord is about to give him. Ezekiel receives a scroll with writings of lamentations, wailing, and woe written on the front and back of it. The Lord instructs him to eat the scroll and then go to speak to the house of Israel. The phrase "the house of Israel" refers to the nation of the Israelites.

When Ezekiel eats the scroll, it tastes as sweet as honey. In the Book of Jeremiah, a contemporary of Ezekiel living in Jerusalem, we read, "When I found your words, I devoured them; your words were my joy, the happiness of my heart" (Jeremiah 15:16). Ezekiel will learn, as other prophets have learned, that sharing the Word of the Lord will be both sweet and bitter.

3:5–27 Ezekiel's Responsibility

Ezekiel is to prophesy to the Israelites in the land of exile, where the Israelites encountered people speaking an unintelligible language. Although the Israelites can understand Ezekiel, they will stubbornly refuse to listen to him, just as they refused to listen to the Lord. The Lord will make Ezekiel just as stubborn as they were. He is not to be terrified by them or their stares, but to continue to proclaim, "Thus says the LORD God!"

As the spirit carries Ezekiel off, his vision ends with the sound of thunderous rumbling as the glory of the Lord, the living creatures, and the wheels depart. He feels anger and bitterness, apparently experiencing the anger and bitterness the Lord has for the rebellious Israelites. He arrives at a place named Tel-abib by the river Chebar, the place inhabited by the exiled Israelites. After seven days, he is still troubled when the Word of the Lord comes to him.

The Word of the Lord informs Ezekiel of his appointment as a sentinel for the house of Israel. "Sentinel" was often used to refer to a prophet whose duty it was to keep watch for the people of Israel. Ezekiel must warn the people for the Lord. If Ezekiel fails to pass this warning on to them, then the Lord will hold Ezekiel responsible for their blood. If Ezekiel warns them and they refuse to turn from their evil ways, then they will die, but Ezekiel will save his own life.

The Lord warns that if those who are just turn to evil when the Lord puts a stumbling block in their way, then they will die. Even if Ezekiel warns them about their sin, they will die and their just deeds will be forgotten. If Ezekiel warns the just to avoid sin and they listen to him, they will live and Ezekiel will, in turn, save his life.

When the Lord instructs Ezekiel to go into the plain where he would experience the glory of the Lord, he goes as directed and encounters the glory of the Lord. He falls prostrate on his face, and the spirit enters him, lifts him up, instructs him to go into his house, and informs him the people will bind him with ropes so he cannot go out among them.

Besides this affliction from the people, the spirit will make Ezekiel's tongue stick to the roof of his mouth so he will become mute, unable to rebuke the people for their rebellious spirit. Only when the spirit speaks to Ezekiel and opens his mouth will he be able to say, "Thus says the LORD God!" The Word of the Lord calls upon those with ears to hear to hear, and those who resist to resist. Those who accept the Lord's message will listen with attentiveness, while those who resist will stubbornly refuse to listen. The Lord notes the house of Israel is a "rebellious house."

Review Questions

1. Why is Ezekiel's vision so confusing to many people, and what is his motive for telling us about such a confusing vision?
2. Why did God tell Ezekiel to eat the scroll? What would that mean to people today who wish to serve the Lord?
3. What does the Lord mean when telling Ezekiel to take the Lord's words into his heart?
4. What does the text mean when it speaks of Ezekiel as a son of man?

Closing Prayer (SEE PAGE 15)

Pray the closing prayer now or after *lectio divina*.

Lectio Divina (SEE PAGE 8)

Relax your body and maintain a posture of prayer (back straight, eyes shut, feet flat on the floor). This exercise can take as long as you want, but in the context of this Bible study, 10 to 20 minutes should be sufficient.

The meditations that follow are provided only to help group participants use this prayer form, but note that *lectio* is intended to bring one to a place of prayerful contemplation where the Word of God speaks to the hearer from his or her heart. (See page 8 for further instruction.)

Ezekiel's First Vision (1)

Ezekiel attempts to describe his heavenly vision, but he can only speak in vague symbolic language, showing an attempt to explain heavenly experiences can never be fully conveyed in human language. The mystics who experienced the presence of God often spoke in symbolic language to describe what had happened to them. People such as St. Teresa of Ávila and St. John of the Cross attempted to explain their experiences of God's presence in their lives, but their explanations remained vague and confusing for many ordinary readers. When people receive a deep spiritual experience, they suddenly discover they cannot express the depth of it in ordinary language. They must often opt to speak as Ezekiel did, saying what it was like rather than what actually happened.

✠ *What can I learn from this passage?*

Eating the Scroll (2—3:4)

When people study and memorize the Bible, they may use the expression, "She (he) devoured the Bible." The aim of this Bible study is to help people devour the Bible and apply its message. Ezekiel's mission is not just to teach the people about the Lord, but to urge them to live the Lord's message. Knowledge of the Bible does not necessarily prove we know its message; it involves meditating on the message of the Lord and living it in our life. If we do this, we are devouring the Word of the Lord.

✠ *What can I learn from this passage?*

Ezekiel's Responsibility (3:5–27)

A reality of life is that every privilege comes with a responsibility. Ezekiel's call to be a prophet was a privilege, but he had the responsibility under the threat of death of being a faithful sentinel for the Israelites. How they received his message was up to them, but Ezekiel had to preach the message or face dire consequences for himself and the Israelites. Parents, those in the healing profession, teachers, construction and office workers, and many other callings in life come as a privilege, but they also bring responsibilities before God. Just as Ezekiel would stand before the Lord, who will judge how well he fulfilled his responsibilities, so we will have to do the same.

✠ *What can I learn from this passage?*

The Book of Ezekiel (II)

EZEKIEL 4—15

And I will give them another heart and a new spirit I will put within them. From their bodies I will remove the hearts of stone, and give them hearts of flesh, so that they walk according to my statutes, taking care to keep my ordinances. Thus they will be my people, and I will be their God" (11:19–20).

Opening Prayer (SEE PAGE 15)

Context

Part 1: Ezekiel 4—7 Ezekiel acts out the siege of Jerusalem, drawing a picture of Jerusalem on a slate and laying himself in front of it like a wall. The Lord puts on his shoulders the guilt of the houses of Israel and Judah. He is to take a sharp sword and shave his head and beard and symbolically use the hair to show the punishment the Lord will cast on Jerusalem because of the rebelliousness of the people. The Lord will allow Judah to be ravaged and the people scattered among the nations. The day of the Lord, the day of judgment, is coming upon them and the Lord will turn away from them.

Part 2: Ezekiel 8—15 The chapters speak about the abominations taking place in the Temple and the rebelliousness of the people, leading the glory of the Lord to leave the Temple. In anger, the Lord sends out angels to execute the idolaters. God casts a dire judgment on Jerusalem with a promise of restoration for those in exile. Again, acting out his prophecy, Ezekiel symbolically performs actions predicting the exile. No matter what the people do to appease the Lord, the Lord's predicted punishment is irreversible. Jerusalem will become like a useless and burnt vine. In performing his tasks as a prophet, the people will reject Ezekiel because they are not pleased with the Word of the Lord he is sharing with them.

PART 1: GROUP STUDY (EZEKIEL 4—7)

Read aloud Ezekiel 4—7.

4 Symbolic Siege and Exile

In this passage, Ezekiel performs symbolic actions depicting the siege of Jerusalem and the hardships of the exile for the people of the northern kingdom of Israel and the southern kingdom of Judah. The Lord instructs Ezekiel to take a clay tablet on which he is to draw an image of the city of Jerusalem. On the tablet, he is to set up campsites and battering rams, commonly used to force an army's way into a city. As a symbol of a barrier between the Lord and the city, he is to take an iron pan and set it up as an iron wall between himself and the city.

Ezekiel is then to lay siege to the city as a sign for the house of Israel. The symbolism apparently points to the northern kingdom, known as Israel, which the Assyrians destroyed around 721 BC. After the death of Solomon, the Israelite nation broke into two, with the northern kingdom receiving the name Israel and the southern kingdom receiving the name Judah. The Lord instructs Ezekiel to lie down on his left side and bear the guilt of the house of Israel by lying there for 390 days, symbolizing the 390 years the house of Israel spent in exile. The number of days equaling the years of sin found in this passage is confusing, since the number of years the people of Israel were in exile does not match the number found here.

When the 390 days are over, the Lord instructs Ezekiel to bear the guilt of the house of Judah for forty days, the number of years the house of Judah spent in exile. The number forty appears to refer to a single generation rather than an actual number of years in exile. A full generation will pass away in exile. The Lord then instructs Ezekiel to turn his face toward the siege of Jerusalem and with a bared (strong) arm to prophesy that the Lord will bind the people of the city in captivity until they have fulfilled the days of their siege.

Ezekiel describes the destitution of the exile in terms of a shortage of food and drink. He depicts the people as mixing wheat, barley, beans, and grain together in a single pot and making them into bread (which they would not ordinarily do) in an attempt to produce enough bread to feed themselves. The Lord orders Ezekiel to eat this bread for 390 days, the number of days he will be on his side. Each day, he shall consume twenty shekels of food (about nine ounces) and drink a sixth of a hin of water (about a quart).

The Lord directs Ezekiel to bake his bread on human excrement in view of everyone, a visible sign of the uncleanliness and desperation facing the people in exile. The Lord orders the people to dig a hole and cover up their human excrement to protect the people from ritual uncleanliness (see Deuteronomy 23:13–14). Realizing cooking food on human excrement would make him unclean, the prophet objects, saying he has never eaten unclean food, so the Lord allows him to cook his food on cow dung, which was commonly used for fuel.

The Lord will add to the hardship by breaking the staff of bread, a symbolic reference to a broken staff, which is useless as a walking stick. The broken staff of bread refers to the lack of adequate food for the people. The people, because of their guilt, will consume the meager bread and water they rationed out for themselves and gradually become weaker.

5 The Message of the Shaven Hair

The Lord directs Ezekiel to speak an oracle against Jerusalem. He is to shave his head and beard, using a sharp sword as a razor. The sword symbolizes the sword of destruction about to come upon the holy city of Jerusalem. Ezekiel is then to weigh the hair and divide it into three parts, placing a third on fire within the city of Jerusalem. Since Ezekiel is already in exile in Babylon, placing his hair in the city of Jerusalem refers to hair placed on the image of the city drawn on the clay tablet.

The Lord instructs Ezekiel to place a second third of his hair around the city and strike the hair with the sword. The last third is to be scattered in the wind and, after he does this, he is to unsheathe the sword. Having saved a few hairs to follow the Lord's last directive, he ties these hairs to the hem of his garment. These few hairs represent the Israelites remaining in Jerusalem who will escape death during the invasion of the Babylonians in Jerusalem. Some of this remnant, however, will be unfaithful to the Lord and face death. Ezekiel foreshadows this event by removing some of the hairs from his garment and throwing them into the fire. In this way, the flaming anger of the Lord will devour the whole house of Israel.

Since the Israelites pictured Jerusalem as the center of the world as they knew it, Ezekiel declares the Lord has placed Jerusalem in the midst of all the foreign nations. According to the Lord, the Israelites rebelled against the Lord with wickedness greater than any other nation. As a result, the Lord states, "See, I am coming against you!" (5:8). The expression "coming against you" was used by forces about to invade a country. In the sight of the nations, the Lord is about to invade Jerusalem, imposing a judgment upon the people so horrible the Lord will never do this again. The plight of the people will become desperate, causing parents to eat their children and children to eat their parents. The Lord will scatter the remnant in the city to the winds, that is, to other nations.

Due to the abominations of the Israelites in defiling the Temple, the Lord will no longer treat them with compassion. A third of the people will die because of disease or starvation; another third will die by the sword; another third will scatter to the winds, and the Lord will pursue them with the sword. The prophecy of the three portions of Ezekiel's hair will be fulfilled.

The Lord's punishment will last until the Lord's anger ceases and the people realize their punishment resulted from the anger the Lord felt toward them. The Lord will leave the city so desolate that the Israelites will become a terror-filled warning to the surrounding nations. As a further sign of the Lord's wrath, the Lord will shower an increase of deadly arrows of starvation on the people and break their staff of bread as one breaks a walking staff. The Israelites will experience starvation, attacks by wild beasts, disease, bloodshed, and the sword of the enemy. Ending this passage with the words, "I, the LORD, have spoken" (5:17), Ezekiel stresses the Lord's determination.

6 Punishment for Idolaters

The Lord presents an oracle to Ezekiel, instructing him to speak to the mountains of Israel, an expression often used in reference to the Israelites. Ezekiel warns the people the Lord is about to destroy them and their "high places" with the sword. The high places referred to raised platforms found outside the cities on which the faithful Israelites once offered sacrifices to the Lord but which were now used for idol worship. Before the Temple in Jerusalem became the sole central place for worship, the faithful used these high places to worship the Lord.

Ezekiel prophesies the Lord will destroy the high places, smash their altars and incense stands, throw down the corpses of the Israelites worshiping the idols, and scatter their bones around their altars. To the Israelites, exposed corpses and bones would desecrate the high places. The Lord proclaims wherever the idolaters live, their cities shall be ravaged; their high places laid waste; and their altars, idols, and incense smashed to pieces. When the slain fall in their midst, the Lord declares they will know, "I am the LORD." From this point onward, this expression or a slight variation of it will be used sixty times in Ezekiel.

The Lord will spare some of the people who lusted after foreign gods, allowing them to live as refugees among the nations of their exile. They will loathe themselves for all their evil abominations and will realize the Lord did not threaten in vain to inflict evil upon them.

Ezekiel delivers a new prophecy from the Lord, instructing the Israelites to clap their hands, stamp their feet, and mourn for all the evils of the house of Israel. Those far away shall die of disease; those nearby shall die by the sword; those spared shall die of starvation. When their slain lie among the idols, around their altars, on every high hill and mountaintop, and beneath every green tree and leafy oak, the people will know the

Lord of the Israelites is truly the Lord. Trees were often identified with fertility gods and idol worship. The Lord will make the land desolate, from the wilderness to Riblah, which is used as a reference to the whole land.

7 The End Has Come

Since the first oracle speaks about the destruction of Jerusalem, the second about the destruction of mountains, the third will now speak about the destruction of the whole land. The Lord instructs Ezekiel to inform the people of Judah their end is about to come from all corners of the earth. Because of the abominations of the people, the Lord will judge them according to their actions, refusing to show them pity. The end will come, leaving no one to cry out joyfully on the mountains.

The crisis arrives as lawlessness reigns and the violent wields the scepter of wickedness. Since all lack innocence, none of the people and nothing of their wealth shall remain. At one time, the daily activities of buying and selling were important, but on the day of crisis, they will no longer be important. Because of their guilt, all will die. When the trumpet sounds the call to arms, no one will go out to battle. Those outside in the field will die by the sword, and those who remain in the city will die by disease and hunger. If survivors flee, they will die in terror in the mountains. Ezekiel speaks of their hands hanging limp and their knees turning to water, both signs of the extreme terror experienced by the people. They will clothe themselves in sackcloth, and shave their heads, signs of shame and mourning.

When the people of Israel worshiped false gods, they would adorn them with silver and gold. Now they will consider silver and gold as useless, throwing them into the streets and treating them as unclean. They can no longer fill themselves with food offered to the gods, which has now become the source of their guilt.

The Lord will abandon the people to foreigners as plunder, and the Lord's house, the Temple in Jerusalem, will be defiled. The worst of the nations (Babylon) shall take possession of their houses. Nothing will be left for them. The king, the prince, and all the people will tremble in fear. The Lord will pass judgment on the people in accord with their actions.

Review Questions

1. What is the message of Ezekiel's symbolic act of the siege of Jerusalem?
2. What does the symbolic action of Ezekiel's division of hair mean?
3. Why will the Israelites experience loathing and remorse when the people are scattered among the nations?
4. Why does God bring disaster on Jerusalem and the cities of Judah?

Closing Prayer (SEE PAGE 15)

Pray the closing prayer now or after *lectio divina*.

Lectio Divina (SEE PAGE 8)

Relax your body and maintain a posture of prayer (back straight, eyes shut, feet flat on the floor). This exercise can take as long as you want, but in the context of this Bible study, 10 to 20 minutes should be sufficient.

The meditations that follow are provided only to help group participants use this prayer form, but note that *lectio* is intended to bring one to a place of prayerful contemplation where the Word of God speaks to the hearer from his or her heart. (See page 8 for further instruction.)

Symbolic Siege and Exile (4)

In Matthew's Gospel, Jesus states "blasphemy against the Spirit will not be forgiven" (Matthew 12:31). The people of Jerusalem provide a perfect example of the unforgivable sin. The sin is unforgivable because a person hardens his or her heart against the message of God. God provides the message and the grace necessary to accept the message, and a person must be open to accepting the message of the Spirit of God. It is not God who makes the sin unforgivable but the person. God was willing to forgive the Israelite nation, but they refused to accept God's message in their life, so God allowed them to be punished for their hardheartedness.

✠ *What can I learn from this passage?*

The Message of the Shaven Hair (5)

In this passage in Ezekiel, the Lord appears so wrathful and ruthless that some later readers draw the image of God in the Old Testament as a punishing and angry God. As we read the total message of the Old Testament, however, we learn God's motive in punishing the people is to preserve the nation from falling into idolatry and to help them repent of their sins against the covenant made with God by their ancestors. Jesus expresses God's true feelings concerning Jerusalem when he weeps over the city because of its impending destruction by the Romans (see Luke 19:41–44). The Scriptures reveal the wrath of God can quickly turn to compassion when people seek forgiveness. Many Old Testament passages portray God as a loving God who pursues creatures with great love, as evidenced in the Book of the Song of Songs.

✠ *What can I learn from this passage?*

Punishment for Idolaters (6)

Even earlier than Ezekiel, the Lord showed a desire for the love and praise of people, especially when they realized the abundant gifts given by the Lord. We, however, encounter so many idols on our journey that make it difficult to remain faithful to all the Lord asks of us. The people of ancient times worshiped false gods along with the one God of Israel just to be sure none of the false gods would become angry if they were overlooked. The people were simply looking for security. In our world today, many people trust the Lord, but sometimes they feel a need for greater security, so they worship the gods of greed, even if it means ignoring the needs of others or hurting them. We can all challenge ourselves every now and then by asking, "Who are the idols in my life?"

✠ *What can I learn from this passage?*

The End Has Come (7)

When disaster occurs in the life of some people, they pray and bargain with God, promising to live a better or more prayerful life, but once the danger has passed, they often forget about the promises they made. When the Israelites faced national tragedies or death, they made promises about changing their manner of life. They realized, however, they often abandoned these promises once peace settled on the land. Now, the Lord treats them as a people whose promises amount to nothing and they must accept the verdict of their own broken promises. The reading challenges us to reflect on the promises we make to the Lord in the course of our life.

✠ *What can I learn from this passage?*

PART 2: INDIVIDUAL STUDY (EZEKIEL 8—15)

Day 1: Vision of the Abomination of the Temple (8)

Ezekiel begins this passage by dating it as the fifth day of the sixth year of the sixth month (September 17, 592 BC). He is sitting in his house in exile with the elders of Judah when the hand of the Lord comes upon him. He sees a figure looking like a man with fire from his waist down and the brilliance of polished bronze from the waist up. The figure stretches out the form of a hand and seizes him by the hair of his head, bringing him in a divine vision to Jerusalem, to an inner gate facing north where the statue of jealousy stood. The statue was apparently a statue to the goddess Asherah, identified with jealousy. Ezekiel is not in Jerusalem, but as he tells us, he is experiencing a vision.

Ezekiel again sees the glory of the Lord he witnessed in the plain when he was struck mute (see 3:22–26). The Lord directs him to look to the north to behold the great abominations the Israelites were practicing. When Ezekiel looks, he sees the place where the Israelites set up the statue of jealousy in the Temple, an action considered to be an appalling abomination of the Lord's sacred sanctuary. Because of this and other abominations, Ezekiel receives the message that the Lord must depart from the Temple. Despite the atrocious abominations already present in the Temple, the Lord informs Ezekiel he is about to witness greater abominations.

The vision continues as the Lord brings Ezekiel to the entrance of the courtyard of the Temple where Ezekiel becomes aware of a hole in the wall. The Lord orders him to dig through the wall and, when he does, he discovers a doorway through which he passes and he sees pictured around the wall figures of every type of creeping things and repulsive beasts. These images represent the many idols of the Israelites.

Ezekiel sees seventy elders of the house of Israel worshiping false gods. Since the vision has taken Ezekiel to Jerusalem, the elders represented here are not the same as those sitting in his house in exile at the beginning of chapter 8. The Lord informs Ezekiel that the elders are worshiping in the dark, thinking the Lord has abandoned the land and cannot see them.

The Lord then brings Ezekiel to the entrance to the north gate of the Temple where women were weeping for Tammuz. The people viewed the withering of leaves and plants taking place in late spring as a sign that Tammuz, a god of fertility, was descending into the abode of the dead. The women, who worship Tammuz, mourn for the false god every year at this time, a form of worship the Lord considers to be an abomination.

The Lord then brings Ezekiel to the inner courts of the house of the Lord and Ezekiel sees twenty-five men between the porch and the altar. They are facing eastward, worshiping the sun with their backs to the altar. The Lord questions whether these abominations are meant to provoke the Lord further. The Lord states they are putting the branch to the Lord's nose. Although the use of the term "putting a branch to someone's nose" is unknown, it appears to be a sign of disrespect. The actions of the twenty-five men cause the Lord to act without compassion, even if they beg the Lord to hear them. The anger of the Lord has reached a point of no return.

Lectio Divina

Spend 8 to 10 minutes in silent contemplation of the following passage:

Ezekiel pictures the Lord as totally alienated from the people, but he knows the Lord is always willing to relent. Throughout the Book of Ezekiel, we hear dire warnings about the destruction of the people, but just when all seems bleak, the Lord adds a word about better days ahead. The Lord we know is a just Lord who punishes those deserving of punishment, but the Lord is also a merciful Lord who does not abandon the people. The Lord is always ready to forgive those who seek forgiveness, no matter how badly they sin.

✠ *What can I learn from this passage?*

Day 2: Slaughter of the Idolaters (9—10)

In chapter 9, Ezekiel hears the Lord cry out in a loud voice for the executioners of the city to come with their weapons of destruction. In the midst of the executioners is a scribe clothed in a linen garment and "with [a] scribe's case at his waist" (9:2). The glory of the Lord moved from the cherub in the holy of holies and went to the threshold of the Temple, symbolically revealing the glory of the Lord had abandoned the most sacred inner room of the Temple. The Lord instructs the scribe to pass through the city and mark an X on the foreheads of those who grieve over the abominations practiced in the city. Behind him, the Lord sends the other executioners, instructing them to strike down without pity every man, woman, and child not marked with an X. Since the Lord instructed them to begin in the sanctuary, the first ones they slaughter are the elders. The Lord orders them to defile the courts of the Temple with the slain and then go and strike the city.

While the executioners are striking the city, Ezekiel falls face down, questioning whether the Lord planned to obliterate all that was left of Israel when the destruction of Jerusalem takes place. The Lord responds that the guilt of Israel and Judah is beyond measuring. Bloodshed and lawlessness ravage the people, leading them to believe the Lord has abandoned the land and no longer sees them. The Lord remains firm, refusing to show pity. Just then, the scribe returns and declares he has done as the Lord commanded.

Ezekiel's vision in chapter 10 describes the Lord's departure from the Temple in highly symbolic terms. He describes something appearing to be a sapphire and a throne above the firmament and above the heads of the cherubim. The image of being above the firmament recalls the image of God placing a dome in the heavens on the second day of creation. The dome separated the water above it from the water below (see Genesis 1:6–7). The people of ancient times viewed the universe as flat with a huge dome keeping the blue waters above the earth from the waters below. They pictured the Lord as enthroned above the dome.

In Ezekiel's vision, the Lord directs the man clothed in linen, the scribe, to go within the wheelworks under the cherubim to gather burning coals with both hands and to scatter them over the city (a symbol of the wrath of God over Jerusalem). When the scribe enters the wheelwork, a cloud, symbolizing the glory of the Lord, fills the inner court of the Temple. The glory of the Lord moves from the cherubim to the threshold of the Temple, filling the entire Temple with the cloud.

Ezekiel then hears the voice of the Lord and sees the glory of the Lord moving out of the Temple. The sound of the wings of the cherubim reaches the outer court, sounding like the voice of God almighty. A cherub puts fire into the hands of the scribe, as a hand appearing to be a human hand is visible under the wings of the cherubim. Ezekiel sees the four wheels beside the cherubim, appearing to be one inside the other and moving in unison in whatever direction the first cherub faced. Eyes covered their entire body, backs, hands, and wings, with eyes covering the wheels. Ezekiel hears the wheels called "wheelwork."

Each living creature has four faces: the face of a cherub, a human being, a lion, and an eagle. When the cherubim rise or stand still, the wheels rise or stand still with them. The glory of the Lord leaves the threshold of the Temple and takes its place on the cherubim, as though on a chariot. When the cherubim rise from the earth with the wheels beside them, they stop at the entrance of the eastern gate with the glory of the Lord above them. These are the living creatures Ezekiel saw beneath the God of Israel by the river Chebar (see Ezekiel 1:1). Ezekiel now recognizes them as cherubim. Their faces are the same as those seen earlier by the river Chebar, and each one goes straight ahead.

Lectio Divina

Spend 8 to 10 minutes in silent contemplation of the following passage:

> When speaking of individuals, Jesus said, "Much will be required of the person entrusted with much, and still more will be demanded of the person entrusted with more" (Luke 12:48). The Lord entrusted much to the community of Israel, but they refused to listen. Because they received many blessings from the Lord and sinned, Ezekiel pictures the Lord as abandoning the Israelite community to their enemies with the hope they would again become faithful to the covenant. We also have received an abundance of gifts from the Lord. We must ask how faithful we are in the use of these gifts and trust the Lord will guide us in the proper use of these gifts.

✠ *What can I learn from this passage?*

Day 3: Prophecies in Exile (11)

The spirit brings Ezekiel to the east gate of the Temple where he encounters twenty-five men, among whom are two men otherwise unknown, Jaazaniah and Pelatiah. The men are planning some type of evil, possibly plotting a rebellion against their oppressors. In recognition of the abandoned homes in the city that the people can inhabit, they tell the people they have no need to build houses. They compare the city to a pot and the people to the meat within it. The pot protects the meat against the fire. The image reflects the mistaken belief that the pot, Zion, cannot fall because of the protective power of the Lord, and the people (the meat) are protected within the city.

The Lord instructs Ezekiel to prophesy against these evil plotters, blaming them for the people slain in the city. They fear the sword, and the Lord will bring the sword against them because of their evil plots, executing judgment against them by handing them over to foreigners. When they experience this judgment, they will recognize it as coming from the one true Lord. The city of Zion will not protect them like the pot protects the meat from the fire. They will experience the judgment of the Lord whose statues and ordinances they did not obey. Instead of following the Lord, they chose to follow the ordinances of the nations around them.

In the vision, while Ezekiel is speaking, Pelatiah drops dead. Since Ezekiel is experiencing a vision, the image of Pelatiah dropping dead did not occur in reality but is a symbolic vision of the sudden death of many people in Jerusalem. Ezekiel, fearing the Lord is destroying all the people of Israel, falls on his face and cries out to the Lord.

The Lord informs Ezekiel that the inhabitants living in Jerusalem view the people in exile as so far away, believing they are now the ones chosen to possess the land. Unknown to them, the Lord plans to reach out to the many who scattered among the nations and found sanctuary in the Lord in these foreign lands, gathering them from the nations of their exile and bringing them back to the land of Israel.

When they return to the land of Israel the Lord gives to them, they shall remove all atrocities and abominations and receive a new heart and a new spirit from the Lord. The Lord shall eradicate from them their heart of stone and replace it with a heart of flesh by which they will walk according to the Lord's ordinances. They will be God's people, and God will be their God. The Lord will bring the conduct of those whose hearts are devoted to atrocities and abominations against them in accord with their deeds.

Ezekiel returns to the vision of the cherubim and the wheels with the glory of the Lord above them. The cherubim rise from the middle of the city and come to rest on the mountain east of the city. The spirit of God then brings Ezekiel back to the exiles in Chaldea where Ezekiel was speaking with the elders in his house when the Lord lifted him up and brought him in a vision to Jerusalem (see 8:1–3). When the vision ends, Ezekiel informs the exiles about all the Lord showed him.

Lectio Divina

Spend 8 to 10 minutes in silent contemplation of the following passage:

The people believed the land was like a pot that protects them from the fire, despite their actions. Some people tend to use something sacred in a superstitious manner. A man who puts a St. Christopher medal in his car and speeds through traffic at a hundred miles an hour, expecting St. Christopher to protect him against an accident, is foolish and superstitious. When the devil tried to tempt Jesus in the desert into trusting God by throwing himself off a high tower in the Temple with the expectation God would save him, Jesus quoted from the Book of Deuteronomy (see 6:16), which stated a person shall not put the Lord to the test (see Luke 4:9–13). The Lord helps those who pray, but the Lord expects them to act with good sense and not expect the Lord to protect them when they are careless.

✠ *What can I learn from this passage?*

Day 4: Prophecy Ridiculed (12—13)

The Word of the Lord speaks to Ezekiel about the rebelliousness of the people who have eyes to see and ears to hear but do neither. They refuse to pay attention to the Lord. In an effort for the people to realize they are a rebellious people, the Lord instructs Ezekiel to pack a bag as though preparing for an exile and to act out going into exile. A bag for exile consisted of one's minimal needs, such as a bowl, mat, and animal skin to hold water. Ezekiel is to do this in the sight of the people, during the day and again in the evening, symbolizing the people will go into exile throughout the day and the night.

The Lord directs Ezekiel to "dig a hole through the wall" and go through it into the darkness, carrying his exile bag on his shoulder. The outer wall of a private home was made of mud, allowing a person to dig through the wall. In this passage, commentators view Ezekiel's digging through the wall as symbolizing a person's desperate attempt to flee from an enemy invasion in the city. Some commentators disagree with this interpretation, viewing Ezekiel as acting out the role of the invaders who breach the walls, not of a single house, but of the house of the city of Jerusalem.

The Lord instructs Ezekiel to cover his face so he cannot see the land. Covering one's face symbolizes shame and grief. By covering his face, Ezekiel becomes a sign for the house of Israel, which will also suffer shame and grief. Ezekiel does as the Lord commands in the sight of all the people.

The Lord tells Ezekiel that in the morning, when the rebellious people of Israel ask Ezekiel what he is doing, he is to announce the load he carries is the prince of Jerusalem (the king) and all people of the house of Israel. Hence, Ezekiel becomes a living symbol for the Babylonians who will carry the people into captivity.

Ezekiel speaks of the prince shouldering his load in darkness and escaping through a hole dug through the wall. The Book of Jeremiah narrates the story of King Zedekiah of Judah, who escapes at night through a gate between two walls only to be captured in the wilderness by the Babylonians and blinded by Nebuchadnezzar, the king of the Babylonians (see Jeremiah 39:1–7). Ezekiel speaks of the Lord spreading his net over the prince (king) who will be captured and brought to Babylon, although he will not be able to see the land, and die there. The Lord will scatter and pursue all the prince's warriors, allowing some to avoid the destruction of the sword, starvation, and plague, so they can share news of all their abominations to these nations who will then know the Lord of Israel is indeed the Lord.

The Lord instructs Ezekiel to eat his bread trembling and drink his water in fear as a sign of the future to the inhabitants of Jerusalem who will eat their bread in fear and drink their water in horror when lawlessness covers the land and the cities and the land are desolate. When the people see this prophecy fulfilled, they will know the Lord of Israel is indeed the Lord.

The Lord addresses the skepticism of the people, recalling a proverb that proclaims the days drag on and every vision fails, meaning life goes on and all prophesies amount to nothing. The people refuse to believe Ezekiel's prophecies, believing the time of the fulfillment of the prophecies will come and go with nothing happening. Jeremiah faced the same type of skepticism when the people declared the prophets are wind and the Word is not with them. In the Book of Jeremiah, the Lord responds that the people will be devoured by fire because of their cynical attitudes (see Jeremiah 5:13–14). The Lord gives Ezekiel a new proverb that declares the days are at hand when every vision will be fulfilled. All false visions and deceitful divinations in the house of Israel shall cease, and that which the Lord speaks will happen without delay. This is an oracle of the Lord.

Along the same line, Ezekiel receives the Word of the Lord which rejects the house of Israel's assertion that the visions and prophecies are a long way off. The Lord declares the Lord's words are final and will happen without delay. This is an oracle of the Lord.

In chapter 13, the Lord delivers oracles against the false prophets. During the period of invasions and threats of destruction for Jerusalem, false prophets arose among the people, predicting peace and victory for the nation. Ezekiel, speaking the Word of the Lord, refers to these prophets as foxes who follow their own whims and see nothing. Like scavenger animals who forage among the ruins for their own survival without caring about others, these false prophets do nothing to fortify the walls around the house of Israel against the day of the Lord's judgment on the people. They dare to declare their oracles come from the Lord, while, in reality, their visions and divinations are false.

The Lord shall punish these false prophets severely, declaring they shall not belong to the community of the Lord's people and will not enter the land of Israel. They shall know the Lord is God of all. They lead the people astray by declaring peace where peace does not exist. When a wall is built, they cover it with whitewash, a type of plaster expected to stabilize the wall. The use of whitewash covers the defects of a wall. Ezekiel, speaking the Word of the Lord, declares the Lord will bring flooding rain, hailstones, and heavy winds that will force the wall to collapse. When this happens, the people will ask what happened to the whitewash the prophets spread on it. The Lord will unleash the rain and hailstones, demolishing the whitewashed wall and leveling it, crushing the false prophets beneath it. There will be no wall, no whitewashers (false prophets). All will recognize the God of Israel is the Lord.

The Lord instructs Ezekiel to speak out against the women who act as prophets, following their own imaginings without hearing the Word of the Lord. Ezekiel delivers the Lord's curse on these women who sell amulets, which are woven for the arm, and veils, coverings for the head. These amulets were used by sorcerers to designate people for life or death. For some barley and bread, they profane the Lord. The Lord declares they intend to use these amulets and veils to preserve the life of those who are evil and who should not live, and death for those who are faithful who should not be slain.

The Lord will free the people from their wicked power, tearing the amulets from their arms and the veils from their heads. They will recognize the God of Israel is the Lord. Because they upset the good people with lies and encourage the wicked not to turn from their evil ways, they shall be destroyed, no longer seeing false visions or practicing divinations.

Lectio Divina

Spend 8 to 10 minutes in silent contemplation of the following passage:

When Jesus was preaching, he often encountered people who refused to accept his message. They heard his voice, but they rejected what he had to say. Like the people encountered by Ezekiel, they had ears to hear, but they refused to listen to the message. Jesus said, "Whoever has ears ought to hear" (Matthew 11:15). The Scriptures tell us about God's relationship with the world; however, we must listen with ears of faith and be open to receiving God's message for it to be of value to us.

✠ *What can I learn from this passage?*

Day 5: Parable of the Vine (14—15)

Elders would come to Ezekiel to consult the Lord, but the Lord knows the elders who visit Ezekiel still worship idols in the silence of their hearts because they do not have these idols with them in exile. They set up a stumbling block between themselves and the Lord. The Lord expresses doubts about consulting with them. The Lord, however, will change their attitudes by speaking to them in such a manner that will capture their hearts. Ezekiel is to encourage them to turn away from their idols and their abominations. If the Israelites or aliens residing in Israel refuse to turn from their sinful ways, the Lord will cut them off from the people of Israel.

The people of ancient Israel believed the Lord could use deception as a means of promoting divine justice. Although the Lord may deceive a false prophet, the Lord will punish the prophet and the one who requested the prophecy so the Israelites will no longer stray and defile themselves by their sin. When the people return to the Lord, they shall be the Lord's people, and the Lord will be their God.

The Lord declares the people of Jerusalem are already condemned because they abandoned the Lord. The Lord poses a situation in which all the people sinned except three worthy people, namely Noah, Daniel, and Job. These three people would save only themselves and not the other faithless people in Jerusalem. The stories of Noah and Job are found in the Bible, but the Daniel in this passage apparently refers to a noble pagan who successfully interceded with the gods and not the Daniel we are familiar with in the Bible. The Lord will send a fourfold punishment, namely sword, famine, wild beasts, and plague against the people, but the Lord will also allow for some survivors. When Ezekiel sees the ways and good deeds of these survivors, he will be consoled, knowing the Lord did not act without a good reason.

In chapter 15, the Lord compares Jerusalem to a vine and its branches. Unlike the tree branches growing wild in the forest, the wood of the vine is good only when it produces fruit. Tree branches, when fruitless, can still be burned for fuel; yet barren vines are useless, fit for nothing but destruction. The ends burn, and the middle remains charred. The Lord declares Jerusalem is faithless, like a vine in the forest that the Lord will leave for the fire. Although some have escaped the fire, the fire will still devour them. Ezekiel, writing from exile in Babylon, knows when the Babylonians burned a large portion of Judah in 597 BC, many escaped and lived, and the Babylonians would return to totally devastate the land in 587 BC. The Lord states the land will be desolate.

Lectio Divina

Spend 8 to 10 minutes in silent contemplation of the following passage:

Jesus referred to himself as a vine and his disciples as the branches. He tells us that by remaining in him, we will bear much fruit, but if we do not remain in him, we will wither and be like branches people gather up and throw into the fire (see John 15:5–6). Ezekiel relates that a barren branch is no better than dead wood found in the forest. The message is clear: If the people of Israel remain faithfully attached to the Lord, they will bear much fruit. Away from the Lord, the branches are useless.

✠ *What can I learn from this passage?*

Review Questions

1. What is the significance of Ezekiel's vision of the abomination of the Temple?
2. Why was the Lord angry with the remnant of Jerusalem?
3. What was the meaning of the symbolic acts of the exile Ezekiel performed?
4. Why did the Lord reject the prophets of peace and the daughters of Israel?

The Book of Ezekiel (III)

EZEKIEL 16—22

Cast away from you all the crimes you have committed, and make for yourselves a new heart and a new spirit (18:31).

Opening Prayer (SEE PAGE 15)

Context

Part 1: Ezekiel 16 The rebellious people have given the Lord the right to destroy them. In turning to other gods, the people have played the prostitute, despite the goodness shown to them and their ancestors by the Lord. The Lord will no longer protect them because they broke the covenant.

Part 2: Ezekiel 17—22 The Lord warns that the king of Babylon will come to Jerusalem and take away its king and officials and bring them to Babylon. The Lord will spare those who are just, but if their son or offspring sin, they will be punished, despite the goodness of the parents. Descendents are not punished for the sins of their ancestors. If wicked people turn from sin, they shall live. The Israelites have a history of infidelities from the time they lived in Egypt before the exile until the present. The king of Babylon shall be against the people of Judah because of the crimes of the people of Jerusalem.

PART 1: GROUP STUDY (EZEKIEL 16)

Read aloud Ezekiel 16.

16 A Parable of Infidelity

The Lord directs Ezekiel to make known to Jerusalem all her abominations, using the image of a woman in referring to the Israelites. Speaking for the Lord, Ezekiel notes the people of Jerusalem had their origin and birth in the land of the Canaanites, with an Amorite father and a Hittite mother, tribes no longer held in high esteem by the Israelites. In a parable, the Israelites are portrayed as a newborn child with an uncut navel cord and a body that was not washed, anointed, rubbed with salt, or wrapped in swaddling clothes. The practice of rubbing salt on the skin of a newborn arose from the belief it would make the skin firm.

From the moment of her birth, no one cared for the child, Israel. She was rejected, abandoned in the field. This image stressed the rejection experienced by the Israelites before the Lord protected them.

The Lord passed by and saw the child (the Israelites) struggling in her blood and said to her, "Live!" The Lord cared for her so that she matured into a woman with breasts and a growth of hair, but the woman was naked. The growth of hair apparently represented pubic hair, which symbolized maturity. When the Lord realized the woman was mature enough for love, the Lord spread the corner of the Lord's cloak over her, a symbol of marriage. In the Book of Ruth, Ruth urges Boaz to spread the wing of his cloak over her as a gesture of marriage, but Boaz declares that another relative has the first right to marry her (see Ruth 3:9–12).

In this passage in Ezekiel, the Lord speaks of swearing an oath and entering into a covenant with the woman. The Lord washed and anointed the woman with oil, clothed her in an embroidered gown and put sandals on her feet, symbolizing she belonged to the family of the Lord. The Lord adorned her with fine jewelry, with gold and silver, and provided flour, honey, and olive oil for her food. Her beauty was admired by surrounding nations, and she was fit for royalty. The symbolism points to the Lord's love, blessings, and concern for the Israelites and their development into a great nation.

When the people of Jerusalem turned to other gods, the Lord addresses them as prostitutes. The woman opened herself to every passerby, worshiping the false idols of the land in which she lived. Being a prostitute, she used the gifts the Lord gave her to establish high places for worship of idols and to make male gods out of her gold and silver. She used her rich clothing to cover her idols, while burning the incense and setting the food the Lord gave her before them. She practiced child sacrifice, immolating and sacrificing the Lord's children in fire before her idols.

In this parable, the Lord alludes to the Israelites who not only worshiped false gods but who also followed the practice of their neighbors in sacrificing their children, a horrible abomination before the Lord. The woman forgot the days when she was stark naked and struggling in blood.

The woman, Israel, imitated the evil ways of others, and she invited others to join in her abominations. She set up a dais at every intersection and spread her legs for everyone who passed by, compounding her prostitution. She served as a prostitute for the Egyptians, identified as having big members, a reference to their sexual stature. The Israelites entered into an agreement with the powerful Egyptian army to fight against their enemies and accepted the worship of the false gods of the Egyptians. As a result, the Lord turned the woman over to her enemies, the Philistines. She went on to prostitute herself for the Assyrians and the Chaldeans (the Babylonians) when she sought their help against her enemies. These countries eventually became her enemies.

When she prostituted herself, the woman sought nothing in exchange for her prostitution. She worshiped the false gods and gave away the gifts the Lord had given to her. In doing this, the woman differed from other prostitutes, who accepted payments for their activities. In a surprising reversal of roles, no one solicited her, but she made payment to her suitors. The prostitute in the parable was replacing her husband with strangers, and, in this case, her husband was the Lord.

The Lord now passes judgment on the woman, saying she lived a life of lust and exposed herself to her lovers, those she loved and those she hated. There were times when the Israelites had to join forces with nations they hated for the sake of defending themselves. Now the Lord will gather all the nations against the prostitute due to her worship of idols and her sacrifice of human life. The Lord will inflict on her the sentence of adultery and murder, which is death, handing her over to the nations and leaving her stark naked. The nations will stone her, set fire to her homes, and inflict punishment on her, putting an end to her prostitution, taking away her ability to offer payment, and turning her own conduct against her. Once all these things occur, the Lord's anger will come to an end.

Quoting the proverb, "Like mother, like daughter," the Lord recalls the woman had a Hittite mother and an Amorite father. She is of pagan background, thus her disdain for giving loyalty to the Lord. Her elder sister was Samaria and her younger sister was Sodom. The people of Samaria and Sodom were relatives of the people of Jerusalem, since they all belong to the family of Abraham, Isaac, and Jacob. As abominable as these sinful nations were, in a short period of time the woman became worse.

The guilt of her sister, Sodom, was not that she had done the abominable acts of the prostitute, but that Sodom and her daughters were proud, complacent with their food, and satisfied in their prosperity, not sharing with the poor and needy. Because of their abominations, the Lord destroyed them. Samaria, the prostitute's sister, did not commit the abominations of the prostitute. Compared to the prostitute (Israel), the sisters, Samaria and Sodom, seem righteous, which should shame the prostitute.

The Lord promises to restore the fortunes of Sodom and her daughters, Samaria and her daughters, and the prostitute, Israel. The prostitute, once proud she was not as depraved as Samaria and Sodom, must now bear her shame and live as a reproach to the Arameans and the Philistines. The woman must bear the penalty of her depravity and abominations.

The Lord will deal with the woman as she deserves in violating the covenant, and the Lord will recall the covenant made with her when she was young and will establish an eternal covenant. Then she will remember her shame. She will receive her sisters as her daughters. The Lord will reestablish the covenant with her so she will know the Lord. She will remember with shame and never again speak when the Lord pardons her for all she has done.

Review Questions

1. Why does the Lord compare the Israelites to prostitutes?
2. Why was the sin of human sacrifice practiced by the Israelites?
3. How does the Lord apply the proverb, "Like mother, like daughter," to the Israelites?
4. How does the covenant affect the Lord's dealings with the Israelites?

Closing Prayer (SEE PAGE 15)

Pray the closing prayer now or after *lectio divina*.

Lectio Divina (SEE PAGE 8)

Relax your body and maintain a posture of prayer (back straight, eyes shut, feet flat on the floor). This exercise can take as long as you want, but in the context of this Bible study, 10 to 20 minutes should be sufficient.

The meditations that follow are provided only to help group participants use this prayer form, but note that *lectio* is intended to bring one to a place of prayerful contemplation where the Word of God speaks to the hearer from his or her heart. (See page 8 for further instruction.)

A Parable of Infidelity (16)

The once arrogant people of Israel were shamed and humbled when they understood how they sinned against the Lord who gave them so many gifts. Sinners, who honestly recognize their sinfulness and repent, know they have no right to disdain others who have sinned or are sinning. The Lord is willing to forgive the Israelites, but the Lord also stresses their need to be ashamed of the sins they have committed. All of us are sinners, and we do not have the right to judge another person's sinfulness.

✠ *What can I learn from this passage?*

PART 2: INDIVIDUAL STUDY (EZEKIEL 17—22)

Day 1: The Eagles and the Vine (17)

The Lord proposes a riddle for the house of Israel. The great eagle (a reference to Nebuchadnezzar, the king of Babylon) came to Lebanon and broke off the topmost branch of the cedar (a reference to the house of David) and brought it to the land of merchants (Babylon). Jehoiachin was the king of Judah who was captured and brought to Babylon in 597 BC. Then the great eagle took some native seed and planted it in fertile soil. The native seed refers to Zedekiah, an uncle of Jehoiachin, who was made king of Judah by the Babylonian king in place of Jehoiachin.

Then another great eagle appeared (a reference to the Pharaoh of Egypt) and the vine (Israel) bent its roots to him. Although Zedekiah swore an oath of loyalty to the king of Babylon, the Pharaoh persuaded him to join forces against Babylon. Zedekiah accepted horses and a mighty army from the Egyptians. The Lord asks in the riddle whether the vine will survive the onslaughts of the east wind, namely the power of Babylon from the east. The vine will wither and die.

The Lord foretells that Zedekiah will not get the help he expects from the Egyptians and will be captured and brought to Babylon. Zedekiah entered into a covenant with the Babylon king, who punishes him for breaking the covenant. The Lord will also bring Zedekiah to disaster for breaking the covenant between the Lord and Israel. Those who flee from Jerusalem with Zedekiah will be captured and killed, except for some who scatter like the wind.

The Lord will then pluck the highest branch from the cedar and transplant it on a lofty mountain of Zion, where it will grow branches and fruit and become a mighty cedar. The Lord is speaking of a revival of the Davidic kingdom, which will bear much fruit and become a mighty cedar, providing a nesting place for the people. Every tree (every nation) will know the God of Israel is the Lord. The Lord will bring low the high tree (Babylon) and lift up the lowly tree (the house of Israel). The green and prosperous tree of Babylon will wither, and the dry tree of Israel will bloom.

Lectio Divina

Spend 8 to 10 minutes in silent contemplation of the following passage:

Parents will often discipline their children with the hope they will grow into stable and healthy adults. Many parents must force their rebellious children to rise early for school, eat the food set before them, avoid eating candy all day, get to bed on time, and accept being "grounded" when they do not cooperate with family rules. In the same manner, the Lord had to discipline the Chosen People who entered into a covenant with the Lord and did not follow the family rules of the covenant. We learn about a merciful and compassionate God when we hear the Lord promising better days for the Israelites after punishing them.

✠ *What can I learn from this passage?*

Day 2: Personal Responsibility (18—19)

The Lord asks Ezekiel the meaning of the proverb that says: "Parents eat sour grapes, but the children's teeth are set on edge." Without waiting for an answer to the question, the Lord, to whom the life of parents and children belongs, teaches only the one who sins shall die. Many Israelites believe the children pay for the sins of their parents, leading them to presume they are being punished for the sins of their ancestors. The Lord instructs the people never again to repeat this proverb.

If a man lives a just life, faithful to the law given by the Lord, he will surely live. Living a just life includes not eating the food of idols on the mountains, not worshiping false idols, not defiling his neighbor's wife, not having relations with a woman during her period, not oppressing anyone, and not robbing. A just life demands payment of debts, feeding the hungry, clothing the naked, refraining from lending money for interest, abstaining from evil, judging fairly between two opponents, and observing the ordinances of the Lord.

If a man begets a son who is violent and commits murder or acts against the law of the Lord, the son will surely not live. His own blood shall accuse him. When the Lord speaks of living and dying in this passage, the reference is not whether a person will physically die but whether the wicked are deserving of the Lord's punishing wrath. When the Babylonians invade Jerusalem, the good as well as the wicked will be killed.

If a father commits sins against the law of the Lord, and the son does not commit sin, the son shall not die for the sins of his father. Only the father who sinned will die because of his sin. Neither the father nor the son will be charged with the guilt of the other. "Justice belongs to the just, and wickedness to the wicked" (18:20).

When a wicked man turns from his sinful ways and keeps the Lord's statutes, doing what is right and just, he shall live. Because of the justice he is now showing, none of the crimes he committed shall be remembered against him. The Lord rejoices in the wicked who turn from their evil ways. In the same way, if a just man chooses evil, he will not live. None of his just deeds shall be remembered.

Some of the Israelites apparently object, saying the Lord's way is not fair. The Lord questions whether or not it is their way, which is not fair. The Lord will judge the house of Israel according to their ways of acting, urging them to reject their wickedness and develop a new heart and a new spirit. The Lord takes no pleasure in the death of anyone.

In chapter 19, the Lord instructs Ezekiel to prophesy a lamentation over the princes (kings) of Israel, using an image of a lioness and her offspring. A lioness raised a young lion who learned to tear apart prey and devour people. The Pharaoh in Egypt captured him and led him away with hooks to the land of Egypt. It was a common practice to drive a ring through the jaw of captives and lead them along by some type of leash. The reference here is to King Jehoahaz of Judah (the lion) who reigned only three months and did what was evil in the sight of the Lord. His mother's name was Hamutal (the lioness), the daughter of Jeremiah (see 2 Kings 23:30–33).

The lioness raised a second lion who learned to tear his prey apart and devour people. At the sound of his roar, all the earth quaked. The nations laid a snare for him and caught him in their pit. They put him in chains and led him away to the king of Babylon. The reference here appears to be Zedekiah (the lion) whose mother was also Hamutal, the daughter of

Jeremiah and the mother of Jehoahaz. Zedekiah died in Babylon (see 2 Kings 24:18—25:7).

The lamentation continues, speaking of a leafy vine as a reference to Judah, once fruitful and full of branches. The "strong branch grew into a royal scepter," an allusion to the house of David (19:11). It grew so powerful it rose among the clouds. But the branch was torn out in rage and thrown to the ground, where the east wind made it wither up. The east wind refers to the destruction imposed by Babylon. The fire spread from the branch to her shoots and devoured it. Judah was no longer the strong vine but a parched land. The royal scepter, the strong branch, is gone.

Lectio Divina

Spend 8 to 10 minutes in silent contemplation of the following passage:

> In the Gospel of John, when Jesus' disciples encounter a blind man, they ask whether his blindness was a result of the man's sin or that of his parents. The belief in those days was any type of physical or emotional ailment came as a result of sin. Jesus declared neither this man nor his parents sinned, thus dispelling the idea the Lord punished people physically because of their sins or the sins of their parents (see John 9:1–3). The punishment endured by the sinners during the time of Ezekiel came as a result of their own sins, as often happens today. For instance, the corruption and idol worship in Ezekiel's day led to the gradual disintegration of the nation. The greed of corrupt leaders of countries in the world today often leads to the gradual decline and destruction of a country.

✠ *What can I learn from this passage?*

Day 3: Israel's History of Infidelity (20)

On the tenth day of the fifth month of the seventh year, which would be August 14, 591 BC, elders come to Ezekiel to consult the Lord, but the Lord refuses to consult with them.

The Lord instructs Ezekiel to remind the elders about the abominations of their ancestors. He is to inform them the Lord chose the house of Israel and swore to lead the descendants of Jacob out of the land of Egypt to the land flowing with milk and honey, a glorious land. The Lord directed the people to throw away their Egyptian idols, but they refused to listen to the Lord. As a result, the Lord became furious and would have destroyed the Israelites in Egypt, but for the sake of the name of Lord, the Lord led them out of Egypt. If the Israelites were totally destroyed, foreign nations would view the God of Israel as weak or no god at all.

In the wilderness, the Lord gifted the Israelites with ordinances to follow and called them to observe sabbaths as a sign between them and the Lord, proving it was the Lord who made them holy. They rebelled, disregarding the statutes and ordinances of the Lord, and grievously violated God's sabbaths. The Lord again became furious and considered destroying them, but for the sake of the name of the Lord, the Lord relented, decreeing instead they would not enter the land flowing with milk and honey.

The Lord then addressed the children of the rebellious Israelites in the wilderness, urging them not to follow the ways of their parents and not to defile themselves with idol worship. The Lord urged them to obey the statutes and ordinances of the Lord and to keep holy God's sabbaths as a sign between them and the Lord their God. When the children rebelled and worshiped idols, they were not destroyed, again for the sake of the Lord's name.

Because of their rebellious spirit, the Lord allowed them to accept statutes and ordinances that were not good and would not give life. The Lord permitted them to become corrupted by offering their firstborn as a fiery sacrifice in order to have them experience disgust and turn to the true God of Israel. In the Book of Exodus, the Lord says, "You shall give me the firstborn of your sons" (Exodus 22:28). Some Israelites may have interpreted this law incorrectly and applied it to the sacrifice of a firstborn. This strict interpretation would make it a statute that was not good and would not give life.

The Lord directs Ezekiel to speak to the house of Israel, saying their ancestors blasphemed the Lord when the Lord brought them to this land. They offered sacrifices, offerings, and oblations to their idols, inflaming the Lord. They made the "high places" a place for idol worship. The high places originally referred to a place of worship on a hill, but it eventually referred to the platforms for worship built by the people. In the face of this defilement by idol worship and sacrificing children, the Lord refused to consult with the house of Israel.

The Lord, the true king of Israel, intends to lead the people into the wilderness for a second wilderness experience and judge them face to face as the Lord judged the people who traveled in the wilderness under Moses' leadership. The reference is to the Babylonian invasion that will scatter the people and leave the land desolate. The Lord will make the Israelites pass "under the staff" and sort out those who defiled and rebelled against the Lord. It was a practice of the Israelites to drive their animals under a staff for the sake of counting them. The imagery points to the Lord as sorting out those who rebelled and who would be destroyed. The covenant will be their judgment rod. Since the judgment of their destruction is already set, the frustrated Lord tells them to go and worship their idols as they wish. Many of the people will be destroyed, but the house of Israel will revive.

The Lord speaks of a new, more joyful development in Jerusalem. On the Lord's holy mountain, the highest mountain in Israel, the whole house of Israel shall worship the Lord. There the Lord will receive praise and the best of the offerings. The Lord will gather the people from among the nations and lands in which they were scattered. The holiness of the Lord will then be evident to the nations. When the Lord brings the people back to the land the Lord promised to their ancestors, the people will remember the ways they dishonored the Lord and loathe themselves in shame. Upon their return, they will realize it is the Lord who brought them back, not as a result of their evil deeds, but for the sake of the Lord's name.

Lectio Divina

Spend 8 to 10 minutes in silent contemplation of the following passage:

The Lord attempted to help the people of Israel by giving them statutes and ordinances that would help them know the Lord's wishes for a holy nation. The Lord also gave them, as the Lord has given us, a free will to obey or disobey the commands of the Lord. Many of the Israelites chose to disobey the commandment of the Lord forbidding people from worshiping false gods. The law is a gift, and our free will is a gift. The two must work together.

✠ *What can I learn from this passage?*

Day 4: The Sword of the Lord (21)

Ezekiel is living in exile in Babylon when the Lord directs him to face south, which is the direction of Jerusalem and Judah. The Lord speaks of the land of Judah as a forest that the Lord is kindling with fire, devouring everything in the land from the south (Judah) to the north (Babylon). When this happens, all people will know the God of Israel is truly the Lord whose fire will not be quenched.

Ezekiel complains the Israelites are accusing him of spinning parables. The Lord instructs Ezekiel to speak plainly of the destruction in Jerusalem by prophesying against its sanctuary and the land of Israel. The Lord draws a sword from its scabbard to cut away from the land the just as well as the wicked. All will realize the sword the Lord has drawn from its scabbard cannot be put back.

The Lord directs Ezekiel to groan bitterly in the sight of the people. When the people of Israel ask why Ezekiel is groaning, he is to tell them it is because of what he heard from the Lord. When the devastation comes, every heart will melt, all hands will helplessly fall, every spirit will become weak, and every knee will be like water. It is coming and has arrived.

The Lord instructs Ezekiel to prophesy about the sword of destruction, already sharpened for the slaughter and honed to flash like lightning. The Israelites rejected the punishing rod and every judgment cast on them. The Lord will not stop now but will turn the polished sword over to the executioner (Babylon).

The Lord bids Ezekiel to cry out and mourn at the devastation of the people and princes (kings) of the Israelites, and to slap his thigh as a sign of grief. Because the people refused to follow the Lord, the Lord punished them. The Lord tells Ezekiel to clap his hands, a gesture equivalent to washing one's hands of any responsibility. The sword will be relentless, striking over and over, filling the hearts of many with fear. At all the gates to the city, the sword will slaughter the people to the right and left. In the midst of this slaughter, the Lord will declare, "Then I, too, shall clap my hands," (21:22) meaning the Lord rejects all responsibility for the punishment the people have inflicted on themselves in abandoning the covenant.

The Lord instructs Ezekiel to craft two roads over which the sword of the king of Babylon may come. Both roads start out from the same land, apparently Babylon. The Lord instructs Ezekiel to place a signpost at the head of each road, with one road leading to the Ammonites, and the other leading to Judah and its fortress, Jerusalem.

When the king of Babylon arrives at the fork in the road, he prepares for the battle by reading the omens that will reveal which road to take. He uses three types of divination. First, he shakes out arrows that tell him the name of the place he should invade. The names of the places were inscribed on the arrows. He then inquires of the teraphim, a household god, and finally he inspects the liver of a newly slaughtered animal and reads an omen in the pattern of the liver. This was commonly done as a form of divination in Mesopotamia, of which Babylon was a part. Into his right hand has fallen the lot marked "Jerusalem," which means the divinations point to Jerusalem. To many of the natives of Jerusalem who consider the once-powerful city of God to be invincible and who had joined with the Babylonian forces, the omen appears to be false. The choice, however, stresses the wickedness found in Jerusalem, which was to be destroyed.

The Lord warns the people of Jerusalem their destruction will expose their guilt, their crimes, and their sinfulness. Death will come for King Zedekiah, a depraved and evil prince of the people who will be deprived of his turban and crown as king. The Lord declares the lowly shall be exalted and the exalted brought low. With the arrival of the king of Babylon whom the Lord is sending in judgment on the people, Jerusalem will be destroyed.

The Lord directs Ezekiel to speak to the Ammonites who were slaughtering people of other nations. The Lord angrily witnessed their arrogance and now casts a fiery judgment upon them. In the past, they destroyed others, but now they will be ravaged with their blood pouring out over the land, making them a forgotten nation.

Lectio Divina

Spend 8 to 10 minutes in silent contemplation of the following passage:

A typical question many people ask is, "Why do the wicked prosper?" In Ezekiel, we read the Lord allows wicked nations to ravage Jerusalem, but in the end, these nations will face total annihilation. Today, we may ask why the wicked prosper, yet we have also witnessed the fall of many evil people, such as Adolf Hitler and Saddam Hussein. Many rich people have wasted away for many years in prison because they cheated others in their attempt to gain greater riches for themselves. The wicked may prosper for a period of time, but their evil ways eventually lead to their downfall.

✠ *What can I learn from this passage?*

Day 5: Crimes of Jerusalem (22)

The Lord directs Ezekiel to judge Jerusalem, which the Lord alludes to as a city of blood and idolatry. Because of the abominations of the people within the city, Jerusalem is responsible for its own destruction. All nations will mockingly refer to Jerusalem as a laughingstock, mocking the city as "Defiled of Name! Queen of Tumult!" (22:5). The people are committing a series of sins explicitly forbidden by the law of the Lord (see Leviticus 18—20). The author enumerates the sins. The kings use their power to shed blood; the people dishonor their fathers and mothers, extort from resident aliens instead of welcoming them, oppress orphans and widows, desecrate the sabbaths, cause bloodshed by slandering, share in feasts in honor of idols on mountains, uncover the nakedness of their fathers, force women to have intercourse during their period, act repulsively with their neighbors' wives, defile their daughters-in-law and sisters by incest, take bribes to shed blood, violently extort interest from their neighbors, and totally forget about the Lord.

The Lord exclaims, "See, I am clapping my hands..." (22:13). Using this symbolic action, the Lord no longer takes responsibility for the people. As a result, the Lord will make them weak and disperse them among the nations to purge them of their filth. Instead of viewing the Lord as weak, other nations will realize the Lord allows these things to happen because of the sins of the people.

The Lord informs Ezekiel the house of Israel has become as worthless as the remainder of melted copper, iron, lead, or silver. Just as these metals are placed in a furnace to be melted with fire and made valueless, so the Lord will chastise the people with the fire of the Lord's anger, leaving them worthless. The people will recognize their plight as resulting from the fury of the Lord.

The Lord instructs Ezekiel to declare Jerusalem to be an unclean land, parched without rain due to the Lord's fury. The city's princes (their kings) are similar to lions tearing apart the people like prey, confiscating their wealth and precious items, and increasing the number of widows. Her priests violate the law of the Lord, not distinguishing between what is holy and what is common, not teaching the difference between unclean and clean, ignoring the sabbaths, and, in general, desecrating the Lord in their midst. Her officials are like wolves tearing apart their prey, shedding blood, and ravaging lives to extort profit.

The Lord speaks of the sins of the false prophets. The false prophets cover all sinfulness "with whitewash, seeing false visions and performing lying divinations" (22:28). Since these fictitious prophets proclaim peace while the Lord attempts to warn the people of the dangers ahead if they do not repent, they often cause problems for the true prophets sent by the Lord.

Although the people continued to cheat, rob, and oppress the poor, the needy, and the alien, the Lord still sought someone who remained faithful enough to save the city from destruction, but the Lord found no one. The Lord's fiery wrath would then devour them, punishing them in accord with their own conduct.

Lectio Divina

Spend 8 to 10 minutes in silent contemplation of the following passage:

During his life on earth, Jesus spoke against some of the Pharisees who rejected his message. They claimed if they lived in the days of the Old Testament prophets, they would not have put the prophets to death, but Jesus accused them of killing the prophets of their own day. He compared them to "whitewashed tombs, which appear beautiful on the outside, but inside are full of dead men's bones and every kind of filth" (Matthew 23:27). The false prophets of Ezekiel's period whitewashed the message of the Lord, ignoring all the spiritual filth within the city. Many people today could tend to whitewash the Lord's message to fit their own sinful manner of life.

✠ *What can I learn from this passage?*

Review Questions

1. Why does the Lord keep relenting and forgiving the Israelites after punishing them for their rejection of the covenant?
2. What is the message of the parable of the eagles and the vine?
3. What is the Lord's message in referring to the proverb, "The parents eat sour grapes and the children's teeth are set on edge?"
4. Give an overview of Israel's history of infidelity.

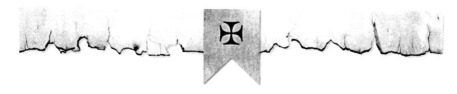

The Book of Ezekiel (IV)

EZEKIEL 23—32

I, the LORD, have spoken; it will happen! I will do it and not hold back! I will not have pity or relent. By your conduct and deeds you shall be judged (24:14).

Opening Prayer (SEE PAGE 15)

Context

Part 1: Ezekiel 23—24 The Lord instructs Ezekiel to speak of the Israelites' worship of false idols in the form of an allegory that presents Samaria and Jerusalem as two sisters who prostitute themselves by giving themselves to other nations and gods. As a result of this sin, these nations, portrayed as lovers, will destroy them.

Jerusalem will be like a pot full of filth placed on a fire ignited for destroying people and for leading the survivors to repentance. Ezekiel's wife dies, and, although he grieves, he remains stoic in appearance. In doing this, he is preparing the people for the day when their grief will be so great they will be stunned and speechless, unable to show external signs of mourning.

Part 2: Ezekiel 25—32 In these chapters, the Word of the Lord comes to Ezekiel with prophecies of doom against foreign nations because of their appalling treatment of the Israelites. The powerful arm of the Egyptian people, who once promised to support the people of Judah but did not, will face disgrace and destruction. The Lord warns Ezekiel that as a specially chosen prophet, he must warn the people of God's wrath or face punishment himself, even when the message is unpleasant. Since the leaders of the people did not shepherd the flock of the Lord (the Israelites) as they should have, the Lord takes the role of a shepherd who separates the good sheep from the bad and punishes the bad.

PART 1: GROUP STUDY (EZEKIEL 23—24)

Read aloud Ezekiel 23—24.

23 The Prostitution of the Two Sisters

The Lord speaks to Ezekiel about two sisters, whose names were Oholah, a symbolic name for Samaria, and Oholibah, a symbolic name for Jerusalem. Since Samaria was the capital of the northern kingdom, which established its own places of worship after breaking from the southern tribes of Judah, the name Oholah, which means "her own tent," is fitting. Since Jerusalem retained the proper place of worship in the Temple, the name Oholibah, which means "my tent is in her," was fitting. The name "tent" refers to the places of worship established in each of the two kingdoms.

Since both kingdoms sought the help of Egypt in their early skirmishes, the Lord portrays them as prostitutes who served Egypt in their younger days, allowing the Egyptians to become closely aligned with them, symbolized by fondling their breasts and caressing their virgin nipples. Since tribes belonged to the Lord, all their offspring belonged to the Lord.

While married to the Lord (a covenant relationship), Oholah (Samaria) lusted after Assyria in all its grandeur and power, lusting after their leaders and their soldiers, handsome young men on horseback. She gave herself to Assyrians as a prostitute by defiling herself with their idols. The symbolism points to the alliance between the northern tribe of Israel and Assyria in earlier battles.

Samaria, however, did not abandon the prostitution she practiced with the Egyptians when she was younger. When Samaria realized the imminent danger she faced against the looming invasion of the Assyrians, she sought help from the Egyptians. As a result, the Lord handed her over to her lovers, the Assyrians, who exposed her nakedness, took away her sons and daughters, and slaughtered them with the sword. The Assyrians totally annihilated the northern kingdom in 721 BC, leading many of the people into exile and causing many others to flee south to Judah.

Although Oholah's sister, Oholibah (Jerusalem), saw what happened to the northern kingdom, she also lusted after the Assyrian army in help against enemies, but Assyria defiled her. The people of Judah became vassals to Assyria. Samaria sought lovers wherever she could to defend herself. She saw images of the mighty Chaldeans (Babylonians) drawn on the walls and lusted after them and sent messengers to them. The Babylonians came to her love couch (land), but they defiled her with their impurities, meaning they ravaged the land. When her prostitution and shame were revealed, the Lord recoiled from her as the Lord did from Samaria.

When the Babylonians threatened the cities of Judah, the Israelites turned to Egypt for help. The Lord views this as Jerusalem entering more deeply into prostitution. The Lord continues to use sexual images to portray the power the Israelites saw in the Egyptian army. He states the Egyptian members were like those of donkeys, and their thrust like those of stallions.

The Lord becomes angry with the people of Jerusalem, saying they returned to the depravity of their youth when the Egyptians fondled their breasts and caressed their young nipples. The Lord will now stir up Oholibah's lovers against her, from Assyria to the cities of Chaldea, who will invade with armor, chariots, wagons, and a multitude of people. The Lord will give these armies the right to cast judgment on the people of Judah and Jerusalem in whatever way they wished. The jealousy of the Lord will allow these armies to deal with them viciously, maiming them and slaughtering them with the sword. Those remaining will be devoured by fire. The enemy shall strip away their clothes and fine jewelry. The Lord will expel their depravity and prostitution from the land of Egypt so they will no longer seek help from Egypt again.

The Lord promises to hand the Israelites over to the hated Babylonians, who will seize all they have, leaving them stark naked, exposing their nakedness to all nations. The Israelites brought this punishment upon themselves because they acted as prostitutes to the nations, defiling themselves with foreign idols.

Because the people of Jerusalem were like the people of Israel (the northern tribes) the Lord will place Samaria's cup in the hands of Jerusalem. The cup in this case refers to the punishment meted out by the Lord. The cup will bring scorn and derision, drunkenness and grief, terror and devastation. The people of Jerusalem shall drink the cup dry, to its very dregs, and they shall tear out their breasts in anguish. This punishment results from the people's abandonment of the Lord. The Lord will now abandon them to their depravity and prostitution.

The Lord calls upon Ezekiel to judge the sisters, Oholah (Samaria) and Oholibah (Jerusalem) and make them recognize their abominations. In choosing other gods in place of the God of Israel, they committed adultery, and they burned their children in sacrifice. They defiled the Lord's sanctuary and desecrated the Sabbath. On the very day they sacrificed their children they entered the Lord's sanctuary and desecrated it. They sent messengers to other nations, luring them to come. For them, they bathed, painted their eyes, put on jewelry, sat on a luxurious couch, and set a table on which they placed holy oil and incense. These lovers (other nations) came to Samaria and Jerusalem as men come to prostitutes. In the end, the just ones shall punish them with a sentence reserved for adulterers and murderers, which is what they are.

The Lord sends out word to bring an army against the sisters and make them endure terror and plunder. Stone them and hack them to pieces, which is the judgment handed out to adulterers. The enemy will kill the sisters' sons and daughters and burn their houses. The Lord will put an end to decadence and all women (nations) will receive a warning not to imitate their depravity. When they pay for their depravity and idolatry, all nations will know the God of Israel is indeed the Lord.

24 Allegory of the Pot

Ezekiel dates this allegory as taking place on the tenth day of the tenth month in the ninth year, which commentators believe refers to January 15, 588 BC. This is the day, according to Ezekiel, when Babylon lays siege to Jerusalem. The Lord directs Ezekiel to preach a parable to the rebellious house of the Israelites.

The Lord tells the people to fill a pot with water and choice pieces of meat, thigh, and shoulder, "the pick of the flock," and boil it, cooking all the pieces. The Lord casts a woe upon the city, comparing the pot to Jerusalem, a city full of blood and full of filth that cannot be removed. The people of Jerusalem are facing slaughter, one by one. The blood of the city is still in the midst of Jerusalem on bare rock. Blood was sacred and uncovered blood was an abomination that called out to the Lord for vengeance.

The Lord casts another woe on the city filled with blood. The Lord will make the pyre great, which means the fire in the city will be massive with the enemy feeding the fire with the plunder and people of the city. Like food being cooked, the people are being killed in the city.

Jerusalem is like a pot that is set empty on coals to heat it up until the pot glows and its impurities melt and its filth disappears. The destruction of Jerusalem is cleansing the city of all its abominations. No matter how great the disaster, the people refuse to amend their ways; the immense filth will not come out of the pot. The Lord must wreak fury on the people. The Lord will not hold back, allowing punishment on the people without pity or without relenting. The people's own manner of life will judge them.

The Lord announces to Ezekiel the love of his life (his wife) will be taken away from him. Despite his grief, he is not to mourn publicly but to put a turban on his head and sandals on his feet and not cover his beard or partake of a mourner's meal. The people know Ezekiel's wife died, but the command of the Lord tells him to live the day in the normal manner.

When the people ask Ezekiel the meaning of his actions, he speaks the Word of the Lord, saying the Lord will now desecrate the Temple, the delight of their eyes, and their sons and daughters will die by the sword. Just as Jerusalem falls so rapidly, they will be like Ezekiel, leaving the turban on their head, sandals on their feet, and not taking part in a post-burial meal with others. They will follow his example by not making these customary gestures of mourning. Instead, they will waste away because of their sins. The number of dead will be so great the people will be numb and speechless, just as Ezekiel was at the death of his wife.

The Lord informs Ezekiel that on the day the Lord takes away the strength of the city, the delight and joy of their eyes, the source of their pride, a survivor will come to Ezekiel, allowing him to hear of the devastation of Jerusalem with his own ears and not from the Lord. Since Ezekiel was brought to exile in Babylon during an earlier invasion by the Babylonians, he is not living in Jerusalem and so does not witness the wreckage of the city and the people. On the day the survivor comes, Ezekiel will no longer be mute and will be able to speak. Previously in the Book of Ezekiel, the Lord struck Ezekiel mute except when he was speaking the Word of the Lord to the people (see 3:26–27).

Review Questions

1. What is the message of the story of the two sisters?
2. What is the meaning of the allegory of the pot?
3. What is the message of the death of Ezekiel's wife?
4. Why does the Lord's wrath turn against Egypt?

Closing Prayer (SEE PAGE 15)

Pray the closing prayer now or after *lectio divina.*

Lectio Divina (SEE PAGE 8)

Relax your body and maintain a posture of prayer (back straight, eyes shut, feet flat on the floor). This exercise can take as long as you want, but in the context of this Bible study, 10 to 20 minutes should be sufficient.

The meditations that follow are provided only to help group participants use this prayer form, but note that *lectio* is intended to bring one to a place of prayerful contemplation where the Word of God speaks to the hearer from his or her heart. (See page 8 for further instruction.)

The Prostitution of the Two Sisters (23)

The allegory of the two sisters who prostituted themselves in breaking their covenant with the Lord offers us a stark and challenging image for our own life. We committed ourselves to the Lord through our baptism, and we renew our baptismal promises each time we celebrate the Eucharist. Few of us would think of ourselves as being like prostitutes when we sin against the Lord and allow the idols of the world to overtake our dedication to Christ. We made a covenant with the Lord, and when we do not keep that covenant we are like people violating a marriage covenant. The lesson challenges us to review our dedication to the Lord.

✠ *What can I learn from this passage?*

Allegory of the Pot (24)

Possibly one of the most difficult moments in Ezekiel's life came with the death of his wife, the delight of his eyes. The Lord allowed him to mourn privately but not to perform any external signs of mourning so as to prepare the people for the bloodbath about to take place in Jerusalem. As Christians, we mourn when someone close to us dies, and we mourn with faith. The Lord knows we must grieve, and unlike Ezekiel, we grieve externally, even as we express our faith in eternal life. We grieve because we can say about the person, "I know I have you, but I don't have you as I had you." Loss of the human presence of a loved one is the source of our grieving.

✠ *What can I learn from this passage?*

PART 2: INDIVIDUAL STUDY (25—32)

Day 1: Prophecies Against Foreign Nations (25—26)

Chapters 25 through 32 include a series of prophecies against foreign nations. When the Babylonians invaded Judah, the surrounding nations took advantage of the weak conditions of Judah and attacked the inhabitants. The Lord seeks vengeance on these nations and those who attacked Judah in earlier periods of history.

The first prophecy uttered by Ezekiel, who speaks the Word of the Lord, involves Ammon, a nation east of Judah. Because they mocked the desecration of the Lord's sanctuary, the destruction of the land of Judah, and the forced exile of the Israelites, the Lord is turning them over to nomadic people from the east who will take over their land, eat their produce, and drink their milk. When these things happen, they will know the Lord of Israel is the Lord.

The Lord speaks against Moab, a nation southeast of Judah, who jeered when the house of Judah fell, viewing it as devastated and weak as other nations. The Lord will allow the nomads from the east to plunder the land of Moab as the Lord did to Ammon, including its three well-fortified cities, wiping away the memory of Moab from the earth. When these things occur, they will know the Lord of Israel is the Lord.

The Lord speaks against Edom, who took vengeance on the house of Judah and occupied a small portion of southern Judah. The fury of the Lord will allow Israel to have vengeance on Edom and destroy the people and beasts of the land, from Teman, noted for its wisdom, to Dedan, noted for its trade. Since the people of ancient times believed conquests came from the hand of a more powerful god, the people of Edom will see in this conquest the hand of the Lord of Israel.

The Lord speaks against the Philistines who maliciously slaughtered the inhabitants in the cities of Judah. The Philistines came from Crete and were known also as Cherethites and seacoast people. The Lord will wipe out a remnant of the Philistines, punishing them furiously. In the midst of this destruction, they will know the Lord of Israel.

In chapter 26, the Lord speaks against the city of Tyre. The prophecy apparently took place shortly before the fall of Jerusalem, speaking now as though it were taking place. Tyre was a commercial center in competition with Jerusalem. Tyre rejoices over the destruction of Jerusalem, because the gateway to trade will now belong to Tyre and not Jerusalem. The ruin of Jerusalem would lead to more profit for Tyre.

The Lord will churn up the nations against Tyre, like a sea churning up waves, destroying its walls and tearing down its towers, leaving it as a bare rock. Tyre was a rocky island, about a half-mile off the mainland, whose destruction would no longer make it useful for trade but only for drying nets on its rocks. Tyre will become plunder for the nations, and her daughter cities on the mainland will be slaughtered by the sword. Nebuchadnezzar, the king of Babylon, would conquer the mainland cities and invade Edom. The Lord speaks of the details of the invasion, the breaking down of the walls and towers, the influx of warhorses, the slaying of the people, the plundering, the destruction of the houses, and the end of music in the city.

The princes of the sea, who are those aligned with Tyre in commercial endeavors, will strip off all their finery and mourn over the loss of such a powerful trading partner. The fall of Tyre makes the nations nearby tremble in fear. The devastation brought by the Lord will leave a ruined city, cast down into the depths of the sea and the world of death, never to return to its glory and power. Despite the devastation recorded in the Book of Ezekiel, Tyre survived the invasion and many centuries later was conquered by Alexander the Great in 332 BC.

Lectio Divina

Spend 8 to 10 minutes in silent contemplation of the following passage:

> The foreign cities invading Judah at the time the Babylonians weakened the land kept their eyes on plunder and not on the power of the Lord of Israel. Although the Lord allowed them to plunder the land, the Lord still had concern for the people of the land. Because of their savagery in plundering the land and the people, the Lord allowed these cities to be invaded and devastated. In our world today, many people forget about the Lord in seeking financial profit

or power, rejoicing when competitors flounder or fail. Jesus knew this would happen, and he urges us to make the Lord our major goal in life. He tells us, "For where your treasure is, there also will your heart be" (Matthew 6:21).

✠ *What can I learn from this passage?*

Day 2: The Ship and Prince of Tyre (27—28)

The Lord instructs Ezekiel to lament over Tyre, an island near the coast that profited both from seafaring ships and from the produce of the coast. The oracle pictures Tyre as a beautiful ship in the heart of the sea adorned with wooden decks and a mast, oars, and a bridge made with materials of major cities known for their fine wood. Its sails were made from the linen of Egypt and its awnings from rich purple and scarlet material. Its oarsmen, sailors, and warriors come from many nations. The city traded with silver, iron, tin, and lead for its wares. Major nations traded with Tyre, exchanging slaves, bronze vessels, horses, and mules. The ship, Tyre, was one of great power and wealth.

After listing the names of many of the nations that traded with Tyre, the Lord predicts a dire end for Tyre. An east wind (Babylon) shatters Tyre in the midst of the sea, sweeping away all its wealth, workers, warriors, and sailors. Those who traded with them mourn, lamenting over the destruction of this once wealthy and powerful nation. The sea was once its source of trade and wealth, enriching the lives of commoners and kings, but now the sea becomes their destroyer as the Babylonians invade them. The nations of the coastlands and their kings lived in dread at the news of the fall of Tyre, while the traders now jeer at this once great nation that has become a horror for all.

In chapter 28, the Lord directs Ezekiel to speak to the prince of Tyre. Although the prince is an image of leadership, he actually represents the inhabitants of Tyre in this passage. With great wealth and prestige, the prince declares he is a god, sitting on a god's throne in the middle of the sea. The Lord tells the prince he is a man, not a god, yet he pretends to be a god, wiser than Daniel (not Daniel the Bible prophet), knowing all secrets.

The prince (all of Tyre) made himself rich through great wisdom and intelligence, heaping up wealth for himself, but his heart became proud. The Lord, reacting to the claim of the prince saying he is a god, will call strangers of the most bloodthirsty nation to come against him. The nation, which is Babylon, will humble the prince (Tyre) and thrust him down into the pit, where he will die a cruel death in the heart of the sea. The Lord asks if he, in the face of death, will claim to be a god. He shall die the death of those who do not follow the law of the Lord. The Lord has spoken.

The Lord instructs Ezekiel to lament over the king of Tyre and to share the Lord's Word with him, reminding the king he was once full of wisdom and beauty and covered with every type of precious stone. The Lord placed him on the holy mountain of God, allowing him to walk blamelessly among the fiery stones from the day he was created until he opened his heart to evil. Walking among the fiery stones referred to walking in the Lord's presence.

In his manner of commerce, the king (Tyre) sinned, so the Lord banished him from the holy mountain and the cherub drove him from the fiery stones. The king had become proud of his beauty and wisdom, and the Lord humbled him, casting him to the ground and making him a spectacle before the kings of other nations. Because of the king's great guilt and wicked trade, the Lord brought fire out of him, a reference to the custom of the Babylonians burning the cities they conquered. All the nations who traded with Tyre were appalled and horrified at the fall of this great nation.

The Word of the Lord spoke to Ezekiel concerning Sidon, north of Tyre, warning the nation the Lord is coming against it. When the Lord delivers judgment on the nation, the people will know the Lord of Israel is the Lord. The Lord will send disease and blood from the sword into its streets. In wiping them away, the Lord will be wiping away thorns and briars tearing at the house of Israel. The surrounding nations will realize the God of Israel is the true Lord.

The Lord speaks to Ezekiel about the days after the exile. When the Lord gathers the house of Israel from the nations among the scattered, manifesting the Lord's holiness through them for all nations to see, then they will live in the land the Lord gave to Jacob, the Lord's servant. The house of Israel will dwell there securely while the Lord executes judgment on their neighbors who treated them with disrespect. Then all nations will know the Lord of Israel is the Lord, God.

Lectio Divina

Spend 8 to 10 minutes in silent contemplation of the following passage:

There is an old saying: "Pride comes before a fall." The reality of life is that all gifts we have come from God, and even the desire and ability to improve those gifts come from God. Knowing the Lord guides us should remove all tendencies toward pride in our lives. The people of Tyre received many gifts, but they became proud. They were powerful, and their pride came before their fall. We should appreciate and wisely use the gifts God gave us, humbly accepting them as a blessing from the Lord.

✠ *What can I learn from this passage?*

___

Day 3: The Lord Deals With Egypt (29—30)

In the tenth year on the twelfth day of the tenth month, which commentators calculate as January 7, 587 BC, the Word of the Lord directed Ezekiel to prophesy against the king of Egypt and all of Egypt. The Lord speaks of Egypt as the great dragon, or sea monster, a mythical god sometimes used to refer to the crocodiles inhabiting the Nile River. Like other powerful nations, Egypt became proud, declaring ownership of the Nile, claiming she created it. The Lord will hook the crocodile, and all the fish of the Nile will cling to its scales, an image of the king and all the people of Egypt being dragged up by the Lord. The Lord will hurl the great beast and all its fish into an open field where beasts of the earth and birds of the sky will consume them. Egypt will recognize that the God of Israel is truly God.

The Lord pictures the king as a cluster of reeds that the house of Israel believed to be strong, but which were actually weak, splintering and easily broken when pressed into battle. The king of Egypt will know the Lord of Israel is truly Lord when the Lord wields the sword against the people and all the animals in Egypt, making the land of Egypt desolate. Because the king claimed to own the Nile, the Lord will turn against Egypt and the Nile and leave the land a dry, desolate waste.

From Migdol (the northeastern limits of Egypt) to Syene (the southern limits of Egypt) to the border of Ethiopia (south of Syene), the land will remain unoccupied for forty years with no human being or beast crossing it. The Lord will make Egypt the most desolate and most deserted of lands, and the Lord will scatter the Egyptians throughout other lands and nations. After forty years, the Lord will bring the Egyptians back to their land, but they will be a weak kingdom, few in number, unable to offer protection to the house of Israel. Their inability to protect the house of Israel will be a reminder to the Israelites of their own sinfulness in turning away from the Lord in seeking support from the Egyptians.

In the twenty-seventh year of the first day of the first month (April 26, 571 BC), the Word of the Lord came to Ezekiel. At the time, Nebuchadnezzar, the king of Babylon, just ended a thirteen-year war against Tyre (587–574 BC), when Tyre finally negotiated to surrender if the Babylonians agreed to take nothing from them. The Babylonians agreed. The Lord, who used the Babylonians as an instrument of vindication against the nations, sent the Babylonians to Egypt to plunder the land in compensation for the years of battle against Tyre.

After the Babylonians finished pillaging Egypt, the Lord promised to make a horn sprout for the house of Israel. A horn often symbolized strength. The image of the horn could refer to a renewal of the Davidic line of kings, or it could refer to the strength the Lord will give the nation. Ezekiel, upon hearing from the Lord that he will have his mouth opened in the midst of the reborn Israel, apparently expects to be alive when the exile ends and the Israelites return home.

In chapter 30, the Lord instructs Ezekiel to call out to the nations to wail when the sword comes to Egypt. The day of the Lord is approaching. The term "the day of the Lord" refers to the day of the Lord's judgment. Ethiopia, south of Egypt, and other nations, once allies of Egypt, shall likewise fall with this once great nation. The pillars of Egypt, a possible reference to the images of the gods, shall fall along with all the Egyptians from north to south. All nations will realize the God of Israel is truly God when they witness the devastation and downfall of Egypt. Messengers from the Lord shall sail to Ethiopia with the terrifying news of the devastation of Egypt, causing fear and distress for the Ethiopians. A river separated Ethiopia from Egypt, making the use of a ship necessary for spreading the message.

The Lord speaks of the devastation of the people and land of Egypt at the hands of Nebuchadnezzar. The Babylonians will fill the land with the slain and the Nile will dry up. The Lord will destroy the idols of the Egyptians and inflict a fiery devastation on the major cities of Egypt (Memphis, Pathros, Zoan, Thebes, Pelusium, On, Pi-beseth, and Tahpanhes). Darkness will cover the land and the women will go into captivity. The Lord will carry out the destruction of Egypt so the nation will know the God of Israel is the Lord.

On the seventh day of the first month of the eleventh year (April 29, 587 BC), the Lord informs Ezekiel about the total destruction of the Egyptian people. The Lord has broken the arm of the Pharaoh, a break that immobilized the arm and was not set. In using the word "Pharaoh" here, the Lord is not speaking about the Pharaoh alone but the whole nation. The Lord will break both arms of the Pharaoh, the one already broken and the other arm so the Pharaoh will never be able to wield the sword again, forcing the Egyptians to drop the sword and scatter to other nations for protection.

The Lord will strengthen the arms of the king of Babylon and place the Lord's sword in the king's hand so he can use it against Egypt for plunder and pillage. When the nations see the Lord has strengthened the arms of the Babylonians and weakened the arms of the Egyptians, they will know the Lord of Israel is truly God.

Lectio Divina

Spend 8 to 10 minutes in silent contemplation of the following passage:

An eighty-year-old man rose early every morning to care for a paralyzed friend who lived three streets away. He would bathe him, feed him, buy his groceries, and sit with him most of the day. When someone asked what gave him the energy to do this, he held up his two arms and said, "As long as the Lord keeps me strong, I want to do this for my friend who did so much for me before he was paralyzed." Ezekiel uses the symbolic image of the Lord breaking the arms of the Egyptians to show how weak the country had become. Unlike the eighty-year-old man, Israel was not strong enough to help Egypt. Some of us are strong enough to help those in need, and some of us are not. Jesus told us those of us who have physical, financial, emotional, or spiritual strength should use these gifts to help others in need. The Lord has given us strength to perform many good actions in our lives. We must use our strength for the Lord.

✠ *What can I learn from this passage?*

Day 4: Lament Over the Pharaoh (31—32)

On the first day of the third month in the eleventh year (June 21, 587 BC), the Lord instructs Ezekiel to ask Pharaoh, the king of Egypt, and the Egyptians whom they are like in their greatness. When Ezekiel speaks of the Pharaoh, he is also speaking of the people of Egypt. The Lord is warning the Egyptians they can fall from greatness just as other great nations have fallen. The Lord then speaks of the magnificence and fall of Assyria, describing Assyria as a type of cosmic tree, a cedar of Lebanon with beautiful branches providing shade (protection), towering high in the sky over all other trees, receiving its growth from deep, running waters.

In the branches of this magnificent tree nested all the birds of the sky and under its boughs the wild animals gave birth. In its shade dwelt the smaller trees, mighty but smaller nations. The Lord speaks of this tree (Assyria) as rooted in the Garden of God. Assyria claimed they were responsible for their own greatness, but the Lord stresses they were planted in the Garden of God by the Lord. No other tree (nation) could match it. The Lord made it beautiful, with abundant foliage, making it the envy of all the other trees in Eden, a name that means a "fertile plain."

As great as Assyria was, it would fall. Assyria was arrogant and exalted itself because of its height over the other trees, so the Lord handed the nation over to a ruler of nations, the king of Babylon. The Babylonians and Medes destroyed the Assyrian Empire in a series of conflicts between 614 and 609 BC. These ruthless nations cut down this magnificent tree, leaving its boughs broken and spread in every ravine of the land. It could no longer give shade to its allies. The birds sat on its fallen trunk and the beasts, who once rested in its shade, now lay beside its fallen branches. This happened as an example for others. From now on, no well-watered tree will tower over the others. No nation will stand for long over other nations.

Not only did the tree fall to the ground, but also the Lord sent it down to Sheol, the place of the dead. With the destruction of the tree (Assyria), the currents of the deep dry up and darkness covers the Lebanon forest, making other trees languish. The Lebanon forest was magnificent, providing the best wood. Nations shuddered at the news of the fall of Assyria. When the Lord sent the tree down to Sheol, some other trees (nations) were relieved. The Lord warns many of the best trees in the Lebanon forest will go down into Sheol, a reference to the allies of Assyria who rested in its shade.

The Lord asks Pharaoh which of the trees of Eden resembles Egypt in greatness and glory. Just as Assyria was brought down, so the sword will bring down Egypt to the underworld with all the other trees, among the uncircumcised.

In chapter 32, the Lord speaks to Ezekiel on the first day of the twelfth month in the twelfth year (March 3, 585 BC), instructing him to utter a lament over the Pharaoh. The lament speaks of the Pharaoh in allegorical fashion as being like a lion among the nations, but the Lord adds he is a monster in the sea, churning up and polluting the waters in streams with his feet.

The Lord will capture the monster (Pharaoh) by casting a net over him like a fisherman who hoists up the net. The net refers to the assemblies of armies invading Egypt. The Lord will hurl Egypt (the monster) into an open field where the birds of the air will roost on the monster and beasts will gorge themselves on its flesh. The mountains and valleys will be strewn with the corpses of the Egyptians, drenching the land and mountains with their blood. Darkness will cover the land.

The Lord will bring anguish into the hearts of many peoples. When the Lord brings the Egyptians into captivity and the Lord brandishes the sword in the face of other nations, they will gape with shock, and kings will quake. The Lord gave this sword to the king of Babylon. The glory of Egypt and all its people and livestock will be slaughtered. No human foot or animal hoof will ever again disturb the banks along the waters. The Lord will make the water clear, bringing it back to its original beauty. When the nations witness the devastation of Egypt, they will know the Lord of Israel is truly Lord. The women of other nations will be chanting such a lament over the destruction of the Egyptians.

On April 27, 586 BC, the Word of the Lord came to Ezekiel, instructing him to wail over the people of Egypt along with the women of powerful nations. The Egyptians will descend to the underworld to be laid to rest with the uncircumcised slain by the sword. Many commentators believe the Egyptians practiced circumcision as the Israelites did, making a burial with the uncircumcised abhorrent. Assyria, Elam, Meshech, and Tubal and all their allies once spread terror, but they were slain by the sword and their graves are set in the pit of the dead. They are not sharing with those who died honorably, the warriors who went to Sheol fully armed with swords placed under their heads, and their shields laid over their bones. It was a custom to bury brave and honorable warriors with their weapons. These honorable warriors spread terror in the land of the living.

The Lord predicts the Egyptians will be broken and laid to rest among the uncircumcised. Edom, with all its kings and princes, will be buried with those slain by the sword and will lie among the uncircumcised down in the pit, along with the generals of the north, the Sidonians, and the Egyptians.

Lectio Divina

Spend 8 to 10 minutes in silent contemplation of the following passage:

During the era in which Ezekiel lived, the great nations boasted about their greatness and gloried in their power, looking down on other nations and often invading their territories. In the Book of Ezekiel, we read about the Lord humbling great nations with extraordinary devastation. The book shows the folly of bragging about power and the wisdom of making proper use of the power the Lord gives us. Power and gifts in any form are given for the common good. Jesus told his disciples many great people use their power to wield authority over others. He declares it should not be that way with them, saying, "Rather, whoever wishes to be great among you shall be your servant" (Matthew 20:26).

✠ *What can I learn from this passage?*

Review Questions

1. What did Ammon, Moab, and Edom have in common that made them enemies of the Lord?
2. Why did the Lord speak an oracle against Tyre?
3. What made the Lord turn against Egypt?
4. What is the meaning of the allegory of the cedar?

The Book of Ezekiel (V)

EZEKIEL 33–48

I will put my spirit in you that you may come to life, and I will settle you in your land. Then you shall know that I am the LORD. I have spoken; I will do it (37:14).

Opening Prayer (SEE PAGE 15)

Context

Part 1: Ezekiel 33—34 Chapter 33 introduces a theme of hope for the future. The Lord will send sentinels (prophets) to the people who must fulfill their roles faithfully or suffer the consequences. The Lord has a warning for those who believe they are chosen to live in Jerusalem and possess the land. They will be destroyed. The Lord exhorts Ezekiel to prophesy against the shepherds of the people who are their leaders. In the end, the Lord, as shepherd, will judge between the good and bad sheep.

Part 2: Ezekiel 35—48 The Lord speaks of a regeneration of the land of Judah and the Israelites. Using the image of dry bones coming back to life, the Lord promises to bring the Israelites back to life. Upon their return to the land, all of Israel will become one nation. There will be a new Jerusalem and a new Temple to which the glory of the Lord will return.

PART 1: GROUP STUDY (EZEKIEL 33—34)

Read aloud Ezekiel 33—34.

33 The Prophet as Sentinel

Although the prophets often had to prophesy an unpleasant message to the people, the Lord warns them in this passage they must never stop prophesying the Lord's message to avoid a confrontation with the people. The Lord tells Ezekiel when the people choose a sentinel (a prophet) from among their number, the sentinel must blow the trumpet to warn the people when he sees the sword (warriors) coming. If the people hear the trumpet and are killed because they did not heed the trumpet blast, they will be responsible for their own death. If the sentinel sees the sword coming and does not warn the people and the sword kills someone, the Lord will hold the sentinel responsible for the death of that person.

The Lord appointed Ezekiel as a sentinel for the house of Israel, which means Ezekiel must warn the people when the Lord speaks to him. If the Lord tells Ezekiel to warn the wicked they will die if they do not change their ways and Ezekiel does not warn them, they will die in their sins, but the Lord will hold Ezekiel responsible for their death. If Ezekiel, after receiving a message from the Lord, warns the wicked and they do not heed his warning, they shall die in their sins, but Ezekiel will save his own life.

The Lord instructs Ezekiel to answer the people who say they are rotting away because of the weight of their crimes and sins by telling them the Lord takes no pleasure in the death of the wicked. The Lord longs for them to turn from their sinful ways and live. There is no reason for them to die.

The Lord directs Ezekiel to relay to the people that when the just sin, they shall surely die, while the wicked who turn away from their wicked ways shall live. If the Lord were to tell those acting justly they shall surely live and they sin, believing their just deeds will bring forgiveness, they shall die. Because of their sin, none of their just deeds will be remembered. If the Lord were to tell the wicked they shall die, and they turn away from their sins, they shall surely live. None of their sins will be remembered.

The Lord knows people say the way of the Lord is not fair. The Lord challenges this belief, asking if the Lord's way is unfair or is their way unfair. The Lord will judge each one according to his or her manner of acting.

On the fifth day of the tenth month in the twelfth year of exile (January 8, 585 BC), a survivor comes from Jerusalem with the news the city was taken. Ezekiel, who was struck mute by the Lord and could only speak the Word of the Lord to the people, learned earlier he would be able to speak again when a survivor from Jerusalem brings him the news of the destruction (see 24:25–27). Upon hearing the news, Ezekiel was no longer mute.

The Word of the Lord comes to Ezekiel, telling him the Israelite survivors who remain in Jerusalem believe the land belongs to them, as it once belonged to Abraham. They view this as a natural inheritance from Abraham. The Lord instructs Ezekiel to remind these people of their sinfulness. They eat the food of idols on mountains where idols are worshiped, shed blood, rely on their swords, commit abominations, and defile their neighbor's wife. The Lord predicts those among the ruins shall die by the sword, those in the open field shall be food for beasts, and those in caves among the rocks shall die by plague. The Lord will make the whole land desolate, and all nations will know the Lord of Israel is truly Lord.

The Lord tells Ezekiel about the people who flock to him to hear the latest words coming from the Lord, but do not act upon them. Love songs come from their lips, but in their hearts they seek dishonest profit. They speak loving words, but act otherwise, viewing Ezekiel as an amusing entertainer. The Lord declares when Ezekiel's prophecies are fulfilled, they will realize a prophet was in their midst.

34 Parable of the Shepherds

The Lord instructs Ezekiel to prophesy against the shepherds (the Israelites' leaders). The Lord sends a warning to the leaders who provide for their own needs, drinking milk, wearing woolen clothing, and slaughtering choice animals while neglecting the flock. Because the shepherds do not strengthen the weak, heal the sick, bind up the injured, or bring back those who strayed or were lost, the sheep are scattered and become food for wild beasts. The flock wanders over mountains, high hills, and scatters over the face of the earth. No one cares to search for them. Because the shepherds do not shepherd the sheep, the Lord will remove the sheep from the hands of the shepherds.

The Lord informs Ezekiel about a new Israel. The Lord will be the shepherd who will deliver the sheep from every place where they were scattered on the dark day of the Babylonian invasion. The Lord will bring them back to their own country and pasture them on the mountains of Israel, where they will lie on good grazing land. The Lord will pasture them, giving them rest, bringing back the strays, caring for the injured, and healing the sick. Those who are fat and strong, the Lord will shepherd as their judge, bringing about their destruction.

The Lord will judge between one sheep and another, between rams and goats. The passage recognizes there are some sheep who are not faithful to the Lord. The evil sheep not only grazed in their own field or drank clear water, but also they trampled on other pastures and polluted their waters with their hooves. The Lord will judge between the fat and the lean, those who provided for their own needs while disregarding the needs of others. The Lord will save the flock so that it can no longer be plundered and appoint one shepherd over them: the Lord's servant David. This is a reference to the kingly line of David, implying there will be one king over a united Israel (see 1 Kings 11:38).

The Lord will make a covenant of peace with the flock, ridding the country of wild beasts, allowing the flock to pasture in the plains and sleep in the forests. They shall have an abundance of rain, fruit-bearing trees, crops, and secure dwelling places on their own soil. When the Lord frees them from the power of those who made them slaves, the people will know the power of the Lord of Israel. They shall live in peace, with no more plundering, no wild beasts to devour them, and no one to terrorize them. The Lord will eliminate famine by preparing fields for planting. The people will know they are the Lord's own people, the flock of the Lord's pasture. They will recognize the Lord is their God.

Review Questions

1. What warning does the Lord give the sentinel (prophet)?
2. What does the Lord say about the survivors in Jerusalem?
3. What is the message of the parable of the shepherds?
4. Why does the Lord speak about a separation of the sheep?

Closing Prayer (SEE PAGE 15)

Pray the closing prayer now or after *lectio divina.*

Lectio Divina (SEE PAGE 8)

Relax your body and maintain a posture of prayer (back straight, eyes shut, feet flat on the floor). This exercise can take as long as you want, but in the context of this Bible study, 10 to 20 minutes should be sufficient.

The meditations that follow are provided only to help group participants use this prayer form, but note that *lectio* is intended to bring one to a place of prayerful contemplation where the Word of God speaks to the hearer from his or her heart. (See page 8 for further instruction.)

The Prophet as Sentinel (33)

A group of men were on a fishing trip when one of them suggested they all go to a brothel and "have some fun." Several of the men agreed, but one man said he would not go because it was a sin. When he said this, another man sided with him and said he too would not go because it was a sin. He later informed the man who first objected that he was afraid to speak up, but when the first man objected, he had the courage to do the same. In objecting, the men were like Ezekiel. They were sentinels, prophets for good, who felt a need to object, even if it were difficult. That's what sentinels do.

✠ *What can I learn from this passage?*

Parable of the Shepherds (34)

Although the Lord, the Good Shepherd, has special concern for the flock, the Lord tells us in the Book of Ezekiel that the Lord will separate the good sheep from the bad. In the Gospel of Matthew, Jesus tells the story of a net thrown into the sea that gathers every kind of fish. The gathering of fish represents all those called to the kingdom of God. When the fishermen reach shore, they keep the good fish and throw away the bad (see Matthew 13:47–48). Using an image of the Lord as a shepherd, Ezekiel teaches the same lesson, telling us the Lord will separate the good sheep from the bad, just as Jesus told us the Lord would separate the good fish from the bad.

✠ *What can I learn from this passage?*

PART 2: INDIVIDUAL STUDY (EZEKIEL 35—48)

Day 1: Regeneration of the Land and the Israelites (35—36)

The Word of the Lord comes to Ezekiel with oracles against Mount Seir, a plateau on which the capital of Edom was established and which represents the whole land of Edom in this passage. Just as the Lord devastated Jerusalem as a punishment against the people, so the Lord will now destroy Mount Seir and leave it desolate for its wickedness against the Israelites. When the Israelites were enduring their final punishment at the hands of the Babylonians and were at their weakest point, the Edomites killed many Israelites. The Lord predicts the blood of the Israelites shall cause Mount Seir to become a land of desolation. The mountains, hills, valleys, and ravines will fill with the slain. When this happens, Edom will know the Lord of Israel is the Lord.

Because Edom said the two nations and two lands (Israel and Judah) belonged to them and attempted to take possession of the lands, the Lord will repay them in accord with the way they treated the Israelites. When the Lord punishes them, they will know the power of the Lord.

They uttered many insults against the land of Israel, boasting during the destruction of Judah that the Israelites and the land were given to them to devour. Because they took joy in knowing the whole land of the Israelites was devastated, the Lord will do the same to them. Mount Seir and the whole of Edom will become a ruin. Then they will know the Lord of Israel.

The Lord instructs Ezekiel to prophecy to the mountains of Israel as though the mountains and land of Israel are like human beings, able to understand what Ezekiel is saying. Ezekiel prophesies to the mountains and hills, the ravines and valleys, the uninhabited and plundered ruins, and the deserted cities of the land of the Israelites. Because the land was ridiculed, mocked, and ravaged by the nations who claimed it for their own possession, the Lord, with burning jealousy, speaks against all these nations, especially Edom, who was most helpful to the Babylonians in ravaging the land of Israel. With wholehearted joy and total contempt, they took possession of the Lord's land. The Lord directs Ezekiel to tell the people about the Lord's jealous rage. Because they endured insults from these nations, the Lord swears the nations surrounding the land will bear the results of their own insults.

Ezekiel prophesies the land will sprout branches and bear fruit for the Israelites, who will soon be returning. The Lord will look kindly on the land which will be plowed and planted, a place upon which the Israelites and their animals will multiply, cities be resettled, and ruins be rebuilt. The Lord will resettle the Israelites as in the past, making them more prosperous than they were before. The Israelites will again possess the land, and never again will the land deprive them of their children. Other nations insulted the land, saying it devours people and its own children, but the Lord will deal with these insults so the land will never again listen to the accusations of other nations.

The Word of the Lord came to Ezekiel, reminding him how the Israelites defiled the land with their vile behavior, which the Lord compares to a woman in menstruation. According to the Book of Leviticus, a woman was considered unclean during her menstrual period, possibly because the blood was considered a source of life and the loss of it represented death (see Leviticus 15:19–33).

Because of the sins of idol worship, the Lord scattered the Israelites among the nations. When these nations witnessed the ruin of the Israelites, they declared these were the people of the Lord of Israel, yet they had to leave their land. The presence of the Israelites among these foreign nations was viewed as a defilement of the Lord's name. The Lord, therefore, decided to gather the Israelites from these nations and bring them back to their homeland, not for their own sake, but for the sake of the Lord's holy name. When the nations see the Israelites returning home, they will realize the Lord of the Israelites is truly the Lord.

The Lord will sprinkle clean water over the Israelites, making them clean from all their impurities and idols. In place of the heart of stone of the Israelites, the Lord will infuse into them a new heart and a new spirit, a heart of flesh and a new spirit by which they will walk according to the Lord's statutes and ordinances. They will live in the land the Lord gave their ancestors and they will be the Lord's people, and the Lord will be their God.

In the land of the Israelites, the Lord will make the grain, the fruit of the trees, and the crops in the field plentiful so the people will no longer have to endure insults from other nations due to famine. The Israelites, recalling their vile behavior, will loathe themselves for their sins and abominations; therefore they will know the Lord is not acting for their sake. They will be ashamed and humbled because of their vile behavior.

After the Lord cleanses the people from their guilt, the Lord will resettle the people in the cities, the ruins will be rebuilt, and the desolate land will be tilled. Nations will speak of the land of the Israelites as a Garden of Eden, resettled and fortified. The Lord will multiply the people so they will be as numerous as the sheep brought for sacrifice, a reference to the sheep brought to Jerusalem on Israelite feast days. When the Lord fills the ruined cities with flocks of people, all will know the Lord of Israel is the Lord.

Lectio Divina

Spend 8 to 10 minutes in silent contemplation of the following passage:

In the Book of Ezekiel, we learn the Lord is a God of justice and a God of mercy. Like a parent who punishes a child for disobedience and later forgives the child, the Lord acts in the same manner. When we sin and sincerely seek absolution with the intent of avoiding the sin in the future, we can be confident that the Lord forgives us. Our attitude of a forgiving God has a great effect on our spiritual and physical life. With spiritual healing comes peace of mind.

✠ *What can I learn from this passage?*

Day 2: Vision of the Dry Bones and Two Sticks (37)

The Spirit of the Lord set Ezekiel down in the center of a broad valley filled with bones. The Lord made Ezekiel walk among these extremely dry bones in every direction. The Lord asks Ezekiel if these bones can come back to life, and Ezekiel answers the Lord alone knows the answer to that question. The passage stresses Ezekiel's call to bring hope to those in exile in Babylon.

The Lord directs Ezekiel to prophesy over the bones, telling the dry bones to hear the Word of the Lord. The Lord speaks to the dry bones, beckoning them to listen and declaring the Lord will make breath enter them, thus making them come to life. The Lord will clothe them with muscles, make flesh grow over them, and cover them with skin so they may have life. When this happens, they will realize the Lord of Israel is truly Lord.

Ezekiel prophesies as commanded, and the sound of rattling like thunder erupted as bone attached itself to bone. As Ezekiel observed, the bones were covered with sinews, flesh grew over them, skin covered them on top, but they lacked breath. The Lord then told Ezekiel to prophesy to the breath, calling to the breath to come from the four winds and breathe into these slain so they may come to life. Ezekiel did as the Lord commanded, and breath entered the slain; as they came to life, a vast army stood up. The images of the slain and army symbolize a battlefield.

In the Book of Genesis, in the story of the Lord creating the first human, the Lord uses a two-step process, first making Adam out of the dust of the earth and after that breathing life into him (see Genesis 2:7). This two-step process is found in this passage, when the bones are first built into a full body and then breath is breathed into them. The Hebrew word "rûah" used in the original text can mean spirit, wind, or breath, which allows the original text to use a play on words to heighten its message.

The Lord informs Ezekiel these bones represented the whole house of Israel. Their lives are like dry bones, dried up, without hope, and cut off from all life. The Lord commands Ezekiel to prophesy, telling them the Lord will open their graves and bring them back to the land of Israel. The people will know the Lord is truly the Lord of Israel when the Lord opens their graves and makes them rise. The Spirit of the Lord will bring them to life and settle them in their land. The Lord has spoken.

The Lord directs Ezekiel to take two sticks and write on one, "Judah and those Israelites associated with it" (37:16). When King Solomon's son became king, the tribes of Israel broke into two sections with ten tribes of Israel establishing the northern kingdom named "Israel," and the two tribes in the south establishing the southern kingdom named "Judah." Writing "Judah and those Israelites associated with it" referred to all those who remained in the land of Judah.

On the second stick, Ezekiel is to write the name "Joseph, Ephraim's stick, and the whole house of Israel associated with it" (37:16). Joseph was the father of Ephraim. Ephraim represents the northern kingdom of Israel. When the northern kingdom was destroyed by the Assyrians in 721 BC, many of the Israelites in the kingdom of Israel fled to Judah. Tensions between the two still existed.

The Lord instructs Ezekiel to join the two sticks together so they become one stick in his hand. When he does this, the people ask Ezekiel the meaning of his actions, and the Lord tells Ezekiel to hold the sticks up in one hand in the sight of the people. He is to tell the people the Lord will soon take the Israelites from among the nations to which they were scattered and bring them back to their land, making them one nation in the land of Israel with one king for all of them, never again to be divided into two kingdoms.

The Lord declares the Israelites shall no longer defile themselves with their idols, their abominations, and their transgressions. In this new Israel, the Lord will deliver them from their apostasy, their defection from the faith, and cleanse them so they will be the Lord's people, and the Lord will be their God. David, the servant of the Lord, will be king over them, and they shall have one shepherd (king). The text does not mean the Lord will raise David from the dead, but that those chosen as kings will follow the spirit and line of David. Although they will have a king, the king will still be a servant of the Lord, subject to the covenant.

When they return to their homeland, the Israelites shall be faithful to the ordinances and statutes of the Lord, living in the land the Lord gave to Jacob, the Lord's servant, and in the land in which their ancestors lived. They shall live there from one generation to the next with David, the Lord's servant, as their prince (king) forever. The Lord will make a covenant of peace with them and multiply them. The Lord's sanctuary (tabernacle) will remain in their midst forever. The Lord will be their God, and they will be the Lord's people. Nations will then know that the presence of the Lord's sanctuary in the midst of the Israelites makes them a holy people.

Lectio Divina

Spend 8 to 10 minutes in silent contemplation of the following passage:

An oft-quoted biblical verse, "nothing will be impossible for God" (Luke 1:37), does not mean the Lord will bring people back to life as the Lord did in the story of the dry bones, but it does mean the Lord can breathe new life into our worst moments. The message of the dry bones is not one of a physical resurrection but one about God's ability to bring a new spirit into the lives of those who have lost all hope. Those who feel lost, despondent, or depressed with no hope of change in their lives can still call out to the Lord to put some life on their dry bones. Just when the Israelites may have given up hope of returning to the Promised Land, the Lord breathed new life into them and they suddenly were able to return home. Nothing is impossible for God.

✠ *What can I learn from this passage?*

Day 3: Prophecies Against Gog (38—39)

Chapters 38 and 39 present three prophecies against Gog. The messages of the prophecies are allegories with apocalyptic overtones, possibly summarizing an overview of all past enemies against the Israelites gathered together under the name of Gog. The episode is presented as a final battle with Israel. Since these passages conclude with the Lord's victory, they are meant to encourage the Israelites to place their trust in the power of the Lord.

In the first prophecy against Gog, the Word of the Lord comes to Ezekiel to look toward a mythical leader, Gog, the chief prince (leader) of two major cities far to the north near the Black Sea. He resides in the land of Gog (or Magog). When Gog musters his army against the Israelites, the Lord will turn him around and put hooks into the jaws of his entire army, a common practice used to link one prisoner with another. In preparation for the battle, the Lord will lead Gog out with his armored warriors, horses, and horsemen, all fortified with shield, buckler, and sword, and many of the major enemies of Israel marching with him. He is to prepare, fully mobilized for war, in the service of the Lord.

After many days, the Lord will call him into battle. In the last days, he will invade a people that survived the sword, a people gathered from among the nations where they were scattered, and a people brought back to the once-wasted land of Israel, where they now live securely. Gog, all his troops, and many nations will come upon the Israelites like a storm and a cloud covering the land.

The Lord tells Gog thoughts will come into his mind, thoughts of an evil scheme to attack a land of unprotected villages and people, quiet people who live in safety without walls, bars, or gates. Gog will seek to plunder and pillage the waste places, now filled with the Israelites gathered from the nations and who live at the center of the earth, acquiring cattle and provisions. Many people of ancient times spoke of their homeland as the center of the earth. The rich nations of Sheba, Dedan, and Tarshish and their young warriors will ask if Gog has come to plunder, to capture silver and gold, cattle, and goods.

In a second prophecy against Gog, the Lord directs Ezekiel to prophesy to Gog that he will approach from his faraway place in the north with many people of many nations riding on horses, a mighty army to war against the Lord's people like a cloud covering the earth. In those last days, the Lord will allow Gog to invade the Lord's land so that nations will acknowledge through him the holiness of the Lord displayed before their eyes.

The Lord speaks of Gog as the one the Lord addressed in former days through the prophets of Israel, who prophesied for years that the Lord would allow him to invade the Israelites. On the day Gog comes against the Israelites, the Lord's anger will flare up with jealousy and fiery wrath. The earth will erupt in an earthquake causing all creatures, fish, birds, animals, all creeping things, and all human beings to tremble at the Lord's presence. The mountains shall collapse, cliffs will fall, and every wall will crumble to the ground. The Lord will summon the sword against Gog, with all the swords turned against their comrades. The Lord will pass judgment on him with disease, causing bloodshed, torrential rain, hailstorms, fire, and brimstone to afflict him and the many nations with him. In this way, the Lord will display the Lord's supremacy and holiness, and all nations will come to know the Lord of Israel is the Lord.

Chapter 39 presents a third prophecy against Gog. The Lord instructs Ezekiel to prophesy against Gog, referring to him again as the Lord did in the first prophecy against Gog as the chief prince of Meshech and Tubal by the Black Sea. Although the Lord claims to have urged Gog to attack the mountains of Israel and brought him up from the farthest parts of the north to lead him against the mountains of Israel, the Lord acted against him, making him weak, an action symbolized by striking the bow from his left hand and the arrows from his right. In Israel, Gog, his troops, and all the people with him will fall in an open field and become food devoured by the birds of prey and wild animals.

The Lord will set fire to the land of Gog (Magog) and those who live securely on the coasts. They will know the Lord of Israel is truly Lord. The Lord's holy name will be revealed to the Israelites, and the Lord's holy name shall no longer be profaned. All nations will know the Lord, the holy one of Israel. The day the Lord has decreed is coming.

All the Israelites will go out into the field and set fire to the buckler and shield, the bows and arrows, clubs and spears. Since the people believed these weapons belonged to the Lord and not to them, they burned them. The vast amount of weapons will provide enough material for burning for seven years, relieving the people of their need to gather wood or cut down trees. The people plunder those who plundered them and pillage those who pillaged them.

On the day of Gog's destruction, the army of Gog will be buried in Israel, in the Valley of Abarim (Valley of the Travelers), east of the Dead Sea. Because of the large number of those slain, the burial will block the way of travelers. The area shall be called Hamon-Gog, which means "horde of Gog." It will take the Israelites seven months to bury the dead, seven being a number that appears to be apocalyptic rather than actual. In accord with their code concerning the necessity of burying the dead, all the people will take part in burying the dead. In order to cleanse the land, some men shall receive the charge of passing through the field to bury the bodies of those who remain unburied. They shall search for the dead for seven months. When searchers discover a human bone, they set up a marker beside it, and the gravediggers bury it in the Valley of Hamon-Gog.

After the burial story concerning Gog, another story of a slaughter of the enemies of Judah follows, apparently referring to another battle. In this story, the enemy is not buried. The Lord directs Ezekiel to speak to all the birds and wild animals, inviting them to the sacrificial feast the Lord is preparing for them where they shall eat the flesh of the warriors and drink the blood of princes and all their animals, rams, lambs, goats, bulls, and all fatlings from Bashan. They shall eat fat until they are full and drink blood until they are drunk. They shall be filled at the table of the Lord with horses, charioteers, warriors, and every kind of soldier.

The event will allow all nations to witness the glory of the Lord of Israel when they experience the judgment of the Lord on this powerful army. From that day forward, the house of Israel will acknowledge the Lord as their God. Nations will realize the Lord allowed the house of Israel to go into exile because of their sins against the Lord. The face of the Lord was hidden from them, and the Lord turned them over to the enemy who slaughtered them with the sword. The Lord dealt with them in accord with their uncleanliness and crimes.

The Lord will now reestablish the fortunes of Jacob, restoring the house of Israel. The Lord is zealous for the sake of the Lord's holy name. When the Israelites live securely and unafraid in their own land, they shall forget their shame and disloyalty against the Lord. When the Lord gathers them from the nations and returns them from the land of their captors, nations will witness the holiness of the Lord. The Israelites will know the Lord is God who sent them into exile and gathered them back into their own land. The Lord will leave no one behind. Once they receive the Spirit of the Lord, the Lord's face will never be hidden from them.

Lectio Divina

Spend 8 to 10 minutes in silent contemplation of the following passage:

In these passages, we learn the restoration of the people does not simply mean bringing them back into their homeland, but it also demands a return to a secure place for the Israelites. As Christians, we receive the call to live close to the Lord, and the Lord in turn promises to protect us. Early in the Gospel of Matthew, we read Jesus is Emmanuel, which means, "God is with us" (Matthew 1:23), and at the end of Matthew, Jesus says, "And behold, I am with you always, until the end of the age" (Matthew 28:20). The presence of God with us stands as bookends in Matthew, stressing the point that in turning our lives over to the Lord, we can find spiritual security in trusting Jesus. No matter what happens in our life, we can always live securely in the Lord.

✠ *What can I learn from this passage?*

_____

Day 4: The New Israel (40—48)

Note: *Chapters 40 to 48 consist of laws for the new Israel concerning the new Temple and the new Israel. For many readers unfamiliar with ancient Israelite customs and rituals, the reading can be tedious, difficult, and confusing. The reader may choose to read the chapters in the*

Bible and the following summary, or just the summary. A reflection is
not included with this summary.

Chapter 40 begins in the twenty-fifth year of Ezekiel's exile, at the beginning of the year, on the tenth day of the month (April 28, 573 BC). The
vision in chapters 40—48 becomes difficult to interpret since the original
text by Ezekiel appears to have gone through a number of editorial addi-
tions and changes by later writers. In the vision, the Lord brings Ezekiel
to a very high mountain in Israel where he sees something like a city built
on it. What appears to be a city is the Temple of the Lord. Ezekiel sees a
man who is actually an angel and whose appearance is like bronze. The
man informs Ezekiel that he is to remember what he sees and pass the
information on to the Israelites.

The man takes Ezekiel on a tour of the new Temple for Israel, measuring off each section of the Temple as they travel from one part of its area
to the next. They move from the gates on the east, north, and south to
the outer court, listing the sizes and positions of the rooms, the thick-
ness and height of the walls, and the length of the vestibules. The man
progresses with Ezekiel into the inner court, where the measurements
and description of the area continue.

In chapter 42, the man leads Ezekiel back to the outer court where Ezekiel describes other chambers on three different levels. Although Ezekiel
appears to be receiving the design of the new Temple from the Lord, the
design is not a literal image of a future Temple but one expressing the
holiness of the Lord and the Israelites who returned from exile. It is an
idealized image of the new Temple.

In chapter 43, the glory of the Lord comes from the east, causing Ezekiel to fall on his face in homage. The glory of the Lord enters the Temple
and the Spirit of the Lord lifts Ezekiel up and carries him to the inner
court. The presence of the Lord in the Temple establishes this magnificent
structure as a holy place.

The Lord promises to remain with the Israelites, never more to part.
The Lord orders Ezekiel to describe the Temple to the house of Israel so
they can gather in the presence of the Lord, ashamed of their sinful ways

in the past. The Lord presents Ezekiel with the dimensions for the altar, explaining the manner of sacrifice. These laws for sacrifice repeat many of the laws found in the Book of Leviticus.

In chapter 44, Ezekiel is brought back to the outer gate of the sanctuary facing east, but it was closed. The Lord declares it must remain closed because the Lord, the God of Israel, came through it. The people defiled the Temple in the past by allowing foreigners to enter it, so the Lord decrees that no foreigner shall ever enter the sanctuary, including those who live among the Israelites. The Levites who sinned shall no longer be allowed to serve as priests of the Lord nor touch anything sacred, but they shall be at the service of the Temple and all its work.

The priests who remained faithful, the sons of Zadok, descendants of Aaron, shall be permitted to approach and stand before the Lord (see 1 Chronicles 6:35–38). They served the Temple before the exile and remained faithful in their ministry as priests. The Lord gives laws concerning the garments for the priests, their manner of dress, and when to wear their priestly garments. The Lord provides regulations concerning the trimming of the priest's hair, their need to refrain from drinking wine before entering the inner court, and the prohibition against taking widows as wives. They are to stand as judges, observe all the laws of the Lord, and keep the Sabbath holy.

In chapter 45, the Lord describes how to apportion the land, which includes setting aside of a portion holier than the rest for the Lord. The Israelites are to apportion land for the priests, other parcels for the Levites, sections for the whole house of Israel, and sections for the princes of the people. They must keep their scales honest and tithe as the law demands. They must follow the law concerning the celebration of the Passover.

In chapter 46, the Lord establishes regulations for the Sabbath offerings, adding details concerning the entrance and departure of the king. The people who come to worship should not leave through the same gate they entered when they came to worship. When a king gives a heritage to a son, the son keeps it, but if the king gives a heritage to a slave, it reverts to the king upon the release of the slave. The Lord established the place for the ovens used by the priests to cook the reparation, purification, and grain offerings, and the area for the kitchens where the Temple ministers cook the sacrifices of the people.

In chapter 47, the man brings Ezekiel back to the entrance of the Temple. Water comes from the Temple. Following the directions of the man, Ezekiel wades into the water that begins as a trickle from under the threshold of the Temple. As Ezekiel continues to wade into the water, it becomes ankle deep, then up to his knees, then up to his waist, and finally it becomes a river in which Ezekiel can no longer wade. The man identifies the river as a sign of the life-giving waters flowing out to the people, watering the fruit-bearing trees and abounding with fish. The Lord establishes the boundaries of the land for the New Israel. These reflect the ideal boundaries of the Promised Land (see Numbers 34:3–12). Within these boundaries, Ezekiel is to divide the land among the tribes of Israel and provide a heritage for the resident alien.

In chapter 48, the Lord names the tribes and where they shall receive their heritage. A large second tract of land shall be divided among the consecrated priests, a portion to the Levites, and a portion for the people to hold in common for city dwelling, pasturing, and providing produce for the workers. The remaining track on both sides of the land shall belong to the prince (the king).

The Lord divides the southern portions among the remaining tribes. The Lord names the three gates on the north, the three gates on the east, the three gates on the south, and the three gates on the west, giving each gate the name of one of the tribes of Israel.

Review Questions

1. What promises does the Lord make concerning the rejuvenation of the land and the people of Israel?
2. What is the message of the story of the dry bones?
3. Why is the background for the message of the two sticks important?
4. What does the Lord say about the return of the Israelites to their homeland?

The Book of Daniel (I)

DANIEL 1—6

Blessed are you, O Lord, the God of our ancestors, praiseworthy and exalted above all forever; And blessed is your holy and glorious name, praiseworthy and exalted above all for all ages (3:52).

Opening Prayer (SEE PAGE 15)

Context

Part 1: Daniel 1—2 In chapters 1 to 6, the Book of Daniel contains six tales about Daniel and his dealings with kings in the Babylonian and Persian courts. Daniel interprets the dreams of the kings, warning them about their overthrow, afflictions, or death. Although he incites jealousy among some seeking favor from the king who want him killed, he survives every attempt with the help of angels of the Lord. Most scholars view the tales in Daniel as coming from a collection of ancient stories.

In chapter 1, King Nebuchadnezzar, the king of Babylon, ordered his servant to bring some of the more outstanding youth from among the Judeans to be trained to enter the king's service. Four of them were chosen: Hananiah, Mishael, Azariah, and Daniel. While in training, they requested vegetables rather than food from the king's table, which they considered unclean according to Israelite law. They remained healthy eating vegetables and were found by the king to be wiser than the magicians and enchanters in his kingdom.

The king had a dream. When the wise men of Babylon could not tell the king what his dream was and its meaning, Daniel came before the king and interpreted the dream about a huge statue of gold, silver, bronze, iron, and feet partly iron and partly clay. The statue represents four successive kingdoms and their fall.

Part 2: Daniel 3—6 Chapter 3 describes Daniel and his companions Shadrach, Meshach, and Abednego—they had been given these Babylonian names—being thrown into a fiery furnace for refusing to worship a huge golden statue of a false god. An angel visits them in the furnace and walks around with them in the fire that becomes a cooling breeze. King Nebuchadnezzar praises the Lord of Daniel and his companions.

In chapter 4, Nebuchadnezzar experiences a vision that refers to his becoming insane and the fall and rise of his kingdom. Chapter 5 tells of another Babylonian king, King Belshazzar, seeing a hand writing on a wall in his palace, warning him about his death. Only Daniel is able to read the writing on the wall. Chapter 6 relates the story of Daniel in the lions' den and the protection given to him by an angel. King Darius the Mede orders those who accused Daniel and all their families killed in the lions' den. The king then praises the God of Daniel.

PART 1: GROUP STUDY (DANIEL 1—2)

Read aloud Daniel 1—2.

1 The Food Test

The author of the Book of Daniel speaks of the beginning of the siege of Jerusalem by Nebuchadnezzar, the king of Babylon, as taking place in the third year of the reign of Jehoiakim, king of Judah. The final siege of Jerusalem took place in 587 BC, when Jehoiakim's son, Jehoiachin, was the king of Judah. The Book of 2 Kings speaks of the siege of Jerusalem as taking place after the death of Jehoiakim (see 2 Kings 24:1–4), but 2 Chronicles speaks of Jehoiakim being taken to Babylon (see 2 Chronicles 36:5–8). Since the Book of Daniel was most likely written in the second century, several centuries after the Babylonian invasion of Judah and Jerusalem, it is understandable for the author of Daniel to be confused about the one who ruled when Nebuchadnezzar invaded Jerusalem.

The Book of Daniel says the king of Babylon carried off some of the vessels of the Temple of God to Shinar, which was an ancient name for Babylon and was mentioned earlier in the Bible in the story of the building of the Tower of Babel (see Genesis 11:1–9).

The king of Babylon ordered Ashpenaz, his chief chamberlain, to bring in some members of the royal family and the nobility of Israel to teach them the language and literature of the Chaldeans (Babylonians). Those brought in were to be young men, without any physical defect, handsome, proficient in wisdom, endowed with knowledge and insight and who could fit in well in the king's palace. The king treated them well, providing them with a daily portion of wine and food from the king's table. They would enter the king's service after three years of training.

A practice in ancient times was to educate the youth in the culture, literature, and language of their conquerors to lessen the desire and chance for rebellion on the part of the conquered people. Rewarding the royalty and nobility with a place in the service of the king would appease the conquered people. From among the Judeans, the chief chamberlain chose Daniel, Hananiah, Mishael, and Azariah. The chamberlain changed Daniel's name to Belteshazzar, Hananiah to Shadrach, Mishael to Meshach, and Azariah to Abednego.

Daniel resolved not to defile himself by eating the food or drinking the wine from the king's table. Jewish law forbade the eating of nonkosher food, food that was not ritually cleansed or prepared in accord with Jewish law, but no prohibition existed concerning the drinking of wine. Perhaps the food and wine may have come as an offering to the gods that was then offered to the people. The chief chamberlain, who favored Daniel and had compassion for him, feared David would lose weight, and the king would see him as thinner than the other young men of his age. This would endanger the life of the chief chamberlain.

Daniel told the guardian put in charge of Hananiah, Mishael, Azariah, and him to give them vegetables to eat and water to drink for ten days. It could then be decided how they looked when compared with the other young men who ate from the royal table. He asked the guardian to treat them according to what he saw after this test. The guardian agreed to the request and tested them for ten days, at the end of which they looked healthier and better fed than any of the other young men who ate from the king's table. The steward thus continued to remove the food and wine they were to receive and gave them only vegetables to eat.

The Lord endowed these four men with knowledge and proficiency in literature and wisdom, and to Daniel, the understanding of visions and dreams. The author is subtly saying Daniel and his companions received their training from the Lord, not from those who supposedly trained them.

After the period of preparation determined by the king, the chief chamberlain brought the four before King Nebuchadnezzar. After speaking with them, the king realized no one is equal to Daniel, Hananiah, Mishael, and Azariah, and so they entered the king's service. To any questions of wisdom or understanding the king asked, they responded ten times better than any of the magicians and enchanters of the kingdom. Daniel remained there until the first year of the reign of King Cyrus, king of Persia, who conquered Babylon in about 539 BC.

2 Nebuchadnezzar's Dream

The author begins chapter 2 by dating the occasion of the chapter in the second year of the reign of King Nebuchadnezzar. In chapter 2, the king seems not to know David and his companions.

In chapter 2, King Nebuchadnezzar experiences a dream that disturbs him greatly and causes him to lose sleep. He orders the magicians, enchanters, sorcerers, and Chaldeans be brought to him to interpret his dream. The Chaldeans in this case refer to the astrologers among the Babylonians who made predictions and interpretations by reading the stars. When they all arrive before the king, the king informs them about his dream, saying he will not rest until he knows what it means. The Chaldeans answer the king in Aramaic, and the language switches from Hebrew to Aramaic from this point to the end of chapter 7. Those reading the original language in which the text was written would notice the change in the language, but English readers would not notice any change.

The magicians, enchanters, sorcerers, and Chaldeans are known as wise men in the kingdom. The wise men ask the king to tell them the dream so they may interpret it. The king, however, challenges them to tell him the dream, believing wise men should know the dream without the king describing it. He may have suspected they would make up an interpretation rather than truly interpreting the dream. The king threatens to have them cut to pieces and their houses burnt and made waste if they cannot describe his dream. If they can tell him the dream and its meaning, the king will give them gifts and great honor.

The wise men again ask the king to tell them the dream so they can interpret its meaning, but the king replies that they are bargaining for time since they now know what he has decided. If they do not tell the king the dream, they shall undergo the punishment he has decreed. The king again demanded that they tell him the dream so he can be assured they are clever enough to give the correct interpretation.

The Chaldean astrologers answer that no man could do what the king wants, and no king before had requested any magician, enchanter, or Chaldean astrologer to perform such a feat. They declare the king's request to be too difficult; no one except the gods who are not human could know the dream. At this, the king becomes violently angry and orders the death of all the wise men of Babylon. The king's fierce reaction may provide an insight into King Nebuchadnezzar's impulsive temper. The decree that all the wise men should be slain would include Daniel and his companions.

When Daniel learns of the decree, he discreetly asks Arioch, the chief of the king's guard, what reason the king has for such severe punishment. When Arioch informs Daniel about the king's meeting with the wise men, Daniel requests time with the king so he can interpret the king's dream. Daniel asks his companions—Hananiah, Mishael, and Azariah—to pray that the Lord would reveal the mystery of the dream to him so he and his companions might not be killed with the rest of the wise men of Babylon.

That night, Daniel receives a revelation of the mystery of the dream in a vision. Using a short psalm, Daniel praises God who has all wisdom and power, who changes the times and the seasons, creates and deposes kings, and who gives wisdom to the wise and knowledge to those who are able to comprehend it. Because light dwells in the Lord, the Lord reveals deep and hidden things and knows what is in darkness. Daniel offers thanks and praise to the God of his ancestors because the Lord has given him wisdom and power. He acknowledges the Lord has revealed what he and his companions had asked and made known to them the king's dream.

Daniel went to Arioch, informing him not to kill the wise men but to bring him to the king so he can interpret the king's dream. Arioch quickly informs the king about a Judean exile who can interpret the king's dream. The king asks Daniel, whose Babylonian name was Belteshazzar, if he can tell him the dream and its meaning. In this passage, the king appears not to know Daniel, despite meeting him earlier (1:18–21), indicating the story of the king's dream was a later addition to the book.

Daniel informs the king that although the wise men were unable to describe and interpret the dream, the God in heaven, who reveals mysteries, has shown King Nebuchadnezzar what will happen in the last days. The events predicted refer to the distant future and not to immediate events. Daniel knows the king wonders what will happen in the future, and the Lord, who reveals mysteries, shows him. Daniel states he received the revelation of the mystery, not because he was wiser than anyone else, but so the king may know its meaning.

Daniel explains the dream, telling the king that in his dream, the king saw a large, bright, terrifying statue. Its head was gold, its chest and arms silver, its belly and thighs bronze, its legs iron, and its feet partly iron and partly clay. While the king watched, a stone was hewn from a mountain with no hand visibly cutting it and it struck the iron and clay feet, smashing them to pieces. The iron, clay, bronze, silver, and gold crumbled immediately, leaving them like chaff on the threshing floor, and the wind blew them away. The stone became a great mountain that filled the earth.

Daniel interprets the dream, calling Nebuchadnezzar a king of kings who has received the kingdom, the power, the might, and the glory from the God of heaven. The Lord made the king ruler of all human beings, wild beasts, birds of the air, and all dwelling places. King Nebuchadnezzar and Babylon are the head of gold. Another kingdom, inferior to the Babylonian kingdom, shall take the king's place, then a third kingdom of bronze, followed by a fourth kingdom of iron which shall break and subdue all the rest, just as iron breaks and crushes everything else.

The feet of the statue, made partly of iron and partly of clay, indicates two kingdoms divided from each other yet seeking unity. The kingdoms will be partly strong and partly fragile. The iron mixed with clay indicates that their alliances will be sealed by intermarriage, but they will not remain united any more than iron and clay remain united.

Daniel explains that the God of heaven will establish a never-ending kingdom. That was the meaning of the stone hewn from the mountain without a hand touching it, which broke in pieces the iron, bronze, clay, silver, and gold statue. Daniel ends his interpretation, telling the king this is exactly what he dreamed, and its meaning will certainly happen.

Although the Book of Daniel does not name the kingdoms making up the statue except that of the golden head (Babylon), it is not difficult to follow the progression of the kingdoms. The silver represents the Median, bronze represents the Persians, iron represents the Hellenistic period of Alexander the Great, and the divided kingdoms after the death of Alexander. Two nations (the Seleucids to the north of Judah in Syria and the Ptolemies to the south in Egypt) were of most concern to the Jewish people. They were divided against each other and twice attempted unity through intermarriage. The stone hewn from rock that becomes a mountain refers to the Jews.

After Daniel interprets King Nebuchadnezzar's dream, the king falls down and worships Daniel, ordering sacrifice and incense be offered to him. The king praises the God of Daniel, telling him his God is the God of gods, the Lord of kings, and a revealer of mysteries. Although the king highly praises the God of Daniel, he also treats Daniel as a divine being by worshiping him and offering sacrifices to him.

The king rewards Daniel with a high position, showers an abundance of generous gifts on him, makes him ruler of the whole province of Babylon, and appoints him as chief prefect over all the wise men of Babylon. The king makes Shadrach, Meshach, and Abednego administrators of the province of Babylon at Daniel's request. Daniel himself continues on at the king's court.

Review Questions

1. What does Daniel prove by refusing to eat food considered to be unclean for a faithful Israelite?
2. Why did King Nebuchadnezzar refuse to tell his wise men his dream?
3. What was the message of the king's dream?

Closing Prayer (SEE PAGE 15)

Pray the closing prayer now or after *lectio divina*.

Lectio Divina (SEE PAGE 8)

Relax your body and maintain a posture of prayer (back straight, eyes shut, feet flat on the floor). This exercise can take as long as you want, but in the context of this Bible study, 10 to 20 minutes should be sufficient.

The meditations that follow are provided only to help group participants use this prayer form, but note that *lectio* is intended to bring one to a place of prayerful contemplation where the Word of God speaks to the hearer from his or her heart. (See page 8 for further instruction.)

The Food Test (1)

The knowledge and wisdom of Daniel and his companions did not come from being trained by Babylonian teachers but by the grace of God. A woman asked her pastor, who touched the hearts of so many people when he preached, where he learned this skill. His answer surprised her. He told her he did the best he could with the talent God gave him, but he realized the real work had to be done by the Holy Spirit. He was not preaching to entertain his listeners but to draw them closer to God. He told her, "No human being can do this without the help of the Holy Spirit."

✠ *What can I learn from this passage?*

Nebuchadnezzar's Dream (2)

In his interpretation of the king's dream, Daniel draws an image of the great kingdoms of ancient times and their demise. Each kingdom saw itself as a glorious kingdom, believing it was indestructible and equal to the gods. Some of the kings wanted to be worshiped as a god. We can ask where these proud kingdoms are today. They had their day, but it passed away. The Lord blesses us with gifts, but we can never boast of our gifts, which come from God. We can express our gratitude to the Lord by using our God-given gifts as well as possible for the greater honor and glory of God, but not for our own greater honor and glory.

✠ *What can I learn from this passage?*

PART 2: INDIVIDUAL STUDY (DANIEL 3—6)

Day 1: The Fiery Furnace (3)

King Nebuchadnezzar has a golden statue of gigantic measurements (ninety feet high and nine feet wide) constructed in the plane of Dura and orders all government officials to be summoned to its dedication. Dura means fortress. It was common for kingdoms to have large statues erected to their gods.

When the large number of officials at the dedication stood before the statue, a herald cried out to all the nations that when they hear the horn, pipe, zither, dulcimer, harp, and all other musical instruments played, they must fall down and worship the statue. If they do not, they will be thrown into a white-hot furnace. (In Babylon, being sentenced to death by fire was a known practice.)

Some of the Chaldeans came to the king and accused the three Jews—Shadrach, Meshach, and Abednego—of refusing to worship the golden statue when the musical instruments were played. The king, in a rage, sends for Shadrach, Meshach, and Abednego and tells them all would go well for them if they promise to fall down and worship the gold statue when they hear the music. If they do not, he will cast them into the furnace, believing their God cannot save them. They tell the king that if their God wishes to save them, then it will happen. If not, they will still refuse to worship the king's god or the golden statue.

The king becomes even more enraged and orders the furnace to be heated seven times greater than usual. He orders some of the strongest men in his army to bind Shadrach, Meshach, and Abednego and cast them fully clothed because of the urgency of the order into the furnace. The heat of the furnace is so intense that it immediately devours the men who throw the three into the furnace. The three Jews fall, bound, into the midst of the furnace.

The three Jews walk around in the flames, singing praises to the Lord. Azariah (Abednego) stands amid the fire and prays. He praises the Lord, referring to the Lord as eternally glorious and just, whose deeds are faultless, and who executes proper judgments in the manner of dealing with the Israelites and the holy city, Jerusalem. The people sinned by performing every type of evil and disobeying the commands of the Lord. Azariah states the Lord acted rightfully in handing the Israelites over to their enemies and to the worst king in the world, a reference to the king of Babylon.

Azariah prays a psalm that is an addition to the original Aramaic text of Daniel and found in the Greek translation. The Roman Catholic Church accepted the psalm and the song of praise that follows (verses 34 to 90) as belonging to the inspired books of the Bible, while most other Christian denominations omit these verses in this third chapter of the Book of Daniel.

For the sake of the name of the Lord, Azariah prays the Lord will not abandon the Jews or the covenant. For the sake of Abraham, Isaac, and Israel, to whom the Lord promised to multiply their offspring like the stars of heaven or the sand on the seashore, Azariah prays the Lord will continue to show mercy to the Jews. He notes the Israelites living in exile are far from the practices of their homeland, with no prince, prophet, or leader. They have no way of offering burnt offerings, sacrifices, oblations, or incense, and no place to offer first fruits to find favor with the Lord.

Azariah prays the Lord will receive them as a living sacrifice, with their contrite hearts and humble spirits, as though these were burnt offerings of rams or bulls, or tens of thousands of lambs. He prays for the Lord to deliver them and to shame those who inflict evil on the Lord's servants.

After Azariah's prayer, the king's servants stoke the fire even higher, more than 300 feet above the furnace, causing the Chaldeans around it to be devoured. An angel joins the three men in the furnace, making the furnace feel as though a cool breeze were blowing through it.

Shadrach, Meshach, and Abednego sing a psalm of praise to the Lord with one voice. They praise the Lord, the God of their ancestors. They praise the Lord's name, the Temple, the throne of the Lord's kingdom, and the Lord who knows the depths of the earth. With each blessing, they repeat a refrain, "praiseworthy and exalted above all forever." They call upon all of the works of the Lord to praise the Lord—the angels, the heavens, the waters above the heavens, all powers, sun and moon, stars of heaven, every shower and dew, all winds, fire and heat, cold and chill, dew and rain, frost and chill, hoarfrost and snow, nights and days, light and darkness, lightning and clouds, mountains and hills, all growing on earth, springs, seas and rivers, sea monsters and water creatures, birds of the air, wild and tame beasts, all mortals, Israel, priests of the Lord, servants of the Lord, spirits and souls of the just, holy and humble of heart. After each of the works of the Lord, they repeat the refrain that offers praise and exaltation to the Lord.

The king leaps up in shock when he sees a fourth person walking unbound in the fire and asks his men whether they cast three bound men into the furnace. He asks how he now sees *four* unbound men walking in the fire, and the fourth looks like a son of God, that is, an angel. The king goes to the opening of the furnace and calls Shadrach, Meshach, and Abednego to come out of the fire. When the king and his officials see the men, unharmed and their clothing untouched by the flames, with not even a hint of the smell of a fire, the king shouts out a blessing of praise for Shadrach, Meshach, and Abednego's God, who sent an angel to deliver them from the oven. They trusted their God rather than worship any god except their own God.

The king decrees whoever blasphemes the God of Shadrach, Meshach, and Abednego shall be cut into pieces and his house ravaged. He declares there is no other god who can rescue people like this, and he promotes the three Jews in the province of Babylon.

The king sends a message to all the people praising the signs and wonders which the Most High God accomplished. He praises the God of the Israelites for the signs and wonders performed, for the Lord's kingship, and his kingdom that endures for all generations.

Lectio Divina

Spend 8 to 10 minutes in silent contemplation of the following passage:

Shadrach, Meshach, and Abednego offered a prayer that recognizes all creation belongs to God. It could easily be a form of praise offered by those who have concern for nature. It recognizes that all of creation worships the Lord simply by being. The sun and moon, light and darkness, animals and humans, mountains and hills, and all of the works of the Lord worship the Lord by being there to remind us of the greatness of God. Their very existence blesses the Lord. The Lord is revealed through the Scriptures, but nature itself should reveal the Lord to us. All your works of the Lord, praise and exalt the Lord above all forever.

✠ *What can I learn from this passage?*

Day 2: Nebuchadnezzar's Madness (4)

The chapter begins with King Nebuchadnezzar speaking of himself in the first person. He experienced a terrifying dream and spoke of the images and visions as filling him with fear. The use of the word "visions" appears to point to more than a dream. Some commentators view his visions as apocalyptic visions that most often point to a disastrous outcome. The king sent for the wise men of the kingdom to explain the dream, but, as shown in chapter 2, they lack the ability to interpret the king's dream. He then sent for Daniel, whose name he changed to Belteshazzar, the name of the king's god in whom, he believes, resides the spirit of the gods. This image appears to refer to Daniel's ability to interpret dreams.

The king described his dream to Daniel. In his dream, the king saw at the center of the earth a large and strong tree of great height reaching into the heavens. The center of the earth was an image used by people of ancient times to refer to their own land. Standing at the center of the earth, the tree could be seen by all ends of the earth. The imagery of the top of the tree touching the heavens recalls the story of the building of the Tower of Babel in the Book of Genesis. The people wanted to build a tower with its top in the sky (see Genesis 11:4).

The leaves of the tree were beautiful, its fruit abundant, and it provided food for everyone. The wild beasts found shade under it and the birds nested in its branches. Everyone ate from it. The beasts and birds appear to symbolize the people of the kingdom. The king then saw a watcher, a reference to an angel, coming down from heaven who cried out in a loud voice that the tree should be cut down, its branches chopped off, and its leaves and fruit stripped away. The beasts will flee from it and the birds from its branches, but a stump and its roots shall remain in the ground.

The imagery suddenly shifted from speaking about the tree to speaking about a man who becomes like a beast. The angel continued to cry out, saying the man should be bound with iron and bronze, fed with the grass of the field, and bathed in the dew from heaven (living outside). Let him live with the beasts in the grass of the earth and let his mind change from a human one to the mind of a beast for seven years. The man will become insane, apparently needing to be bound with strong fetters, symbolized by bindings of iron and bronze. The man will remain insane for seven years. This was the decree of the watchers, given by order of the holy ones. The watchers and holy ones were akin to a heavenly council meeting with the

Lord. The decree was given so all would know the Most High is sovereign over human kingship. The Most High can give kingship to whomever the Most High wills, even to the lowest of mortals.

Daniel hesitated, alarmed at what he heard. The king told him not to be dismayed at the meaning of the dream. Daniel expressed a hope the dream is for the king's enemies and not for the king. He informed the king that he (the king) was that majestic tree with its top in the heavens, its abundance of leaves and fruit, its ability to provide food and shelter for wild beasts, and dwellings for birds. Daniel told the king he had become great enough to touch the heavens, and his dominion extended to the ends of the earth.

Daniel then spoke of the holy watcher whom the king saw come down from heaven and order the magnificent tree cut down and destroyed with only its stump left in the ground. The watcher decreed a man would be bound with iron and bronze, bathed only with dew from heaven, living with the wild beasts for seven years. Daniel declared the Most High had passed a sentence on the king, casting him out from human society to dwell with the wild beasts. For seven years, he shall eat grass like an ox and be bathed with the dew of the earth until he knew the Most High was sovereign over human kingship and gave sovereignty to whomever the Most High wills. The punishment aimed at humbling the king, who became proud of his position.

Daniel interpreted the remaining stump as meaning the kingdom shall be preserved for the king once he has learned heaven (God) is sovereign. Daniel advised the king to atone for his sins by good deeds and for his misdeeds by kindness to the poor. If he did this, his prosperity would be long-lasting.

Twelve months later, the king was walking on the roof of the royal palace in Babylon, telling himself the greatness of Babylon was built by his great strength as a royal residence for his grandeur and majesty. While he was saying this, a voice from heaven issued a decree, saying his kingship shall be taken from him and he shall be cast out from human society to dwell among the wild beasts. Like an ox, he shall eat grass until, after seven years, he learns the Most High is sovereign over the kingdoms of humans and gives it to whomever the Most High wills. This sentence took place immediately. He was cast out, ate grass, and his body was bathed with the dew of heaven. This would last until his hair grew like the feathers of an eagle and his nails became like the claws of a bird, symbols of the king becoming a madman.

Nebuchadnezzar, again speaking in the first person, reported that when this period was over, he looked up to heaven, his sanity was restored, and he praised and glorified the Most High as the one who lives forever.

The king prayed a psalm in praise of the greatness of the Lord, proclaiming the Lord's dominion is an everlasting dominion, one that endures from one generation to the next. All who live on the earth are counted as nothing. The will of the Most High is fulfilled in heaven and on earth, and no one can hold the Lord back or ask what the Most High has done.

When the king became sane again and his majesty and splendor returned to him for the glory of the kingdom, his counselors and nobles came to him. He was restored to his kingdom and became greater than before. He praised and glorified the king of heaven, whose works were right, whose ways were just, and who was "able to humble those who walk in pride" (4:34).

The description of the king losing his kingdom for seven years and becoming insane did not happen to Nebuchadnezzar, although some of the message could be applied to the last king of Babylon, who went to stay in Arabia for a long period of time. Because the people did not understand why he left for such a long period, and perhaps due to his unpopularity among some in his kingdom, many began to speak of him as becoming insane. He returned and ruled his crumbling empire as well as he could. Centuries later, when the Book of Daniel was written, the author of this chapter may have heard this folktale and adapted it to Nebuchadnezzar.

Lectio Divina

Spend 8 to 10 minutes in silent contemplation of the following passage:

The author of Daniel was suffering under a king who showed great pride and caused havoc for the Jews. Daniel believed the king of his own era was proud and perhaps insane because of his manner of acting. The real message for all of us rests on the saying, "Pride comes before the fall." Daniel wanted to show the foolishness of pride and the need for humbly trusting and praising the Lord. This theme runs throughout the Book of Daniel.

✠ *What can I learn from this passage?*

Day 3: The Writing on the Wall (5)

King Belshazzar, whom the author mistakenly identifies as the son of Nebuchadnezzar, gave a great banquet for a thousand of his nobles. Several kings ruled between Belshazzar and Nebuchadnezzar. Belshazzar, who actually never became king, was the son of King Nabonidus and acted as regent of Babylon in his father's absence.

Drunk with wine, Belshazzar ordered the servants to bring in the gold and silver vessels brought to Babylon by Nebuchadnezzar when he sacked Jerusalem. The conqueror of a nation usually confiscated the idols of the captives, but the Israelites had no statues of their God, so Nebuchadnezzar took the vessels from the Temple. While Belshazzar and his nobles, consorts, and concubines were drinking from the Temple's gold and silver vessels, they were praising their own gods of gold, silver, bronze, iron, wood, and stone.

Suddenly, the fingers of a human hand become visible and write on the wall of the king's palace. When the king sees this, his face turns pale, his thoughts terrify him, his limbs shake, and his knees knock together. The king shouts for the enchanters, the Chaldean astrologers, and the diviners to be summoned. As found in previous chapters of Daniel, the king makes grand promises about rewarding the one who could read the writing and tell him what it means. He will clothe him in purple, a royal color, give him a chain of gold to wear around his neck, and rank him third in governing the kingdom. The wise men who come in cannot read the writing or interpret it for the king. King Belshazzar becomes greatly terrified and his nobles become baffled.

When the queen heard about the discussion between the king and his nobles, she told the king not to let his thoughts terrify him or his face become too pale. She said there was a man in the kingdom who possessed a spirit of the gods, a man Nebuchadnezzar made chief of the magicians, enchanters, Chaldeans, and diviners due to his brilliant insight and godlike wisdom. Because Daniel, whom the king named Belteshazzar, showed such an astonishing spirit, understanding, and insight in interpreting dreams, explaining riddles, and resolving problems, the king should summon him to interpret what the handwriting means.

When Daniel was brought before the king, the king asked if he was indeed Daniel, one of the Jewish exiles whom his father Nebuchadnezzar brought from Judah. The king told him that he heard of his brilliant spirit and wisdom and informed him about the inability of the wise men to interpret the writing. The king made the same promise of rewards for Daniel that he made to the wise men. Daniel told him to keep his gifts or give them to someone else. He, however, would read the writing for the king and tell him what it means. Later in this chapter, Daniel received and accepted these gifts.

Before reading the writing on the wall, Daniel informed Belshazzar about the Most High God bestowing on Nebuchadnezzar "kingship, greatness, splendor, and majesty" (5:18). Because of this, all nations and peoples of every language dreaded and feared him. He would kill or let live whomever he wished, and he would exalt or humble whomever he wanted. But when he became pompous and arrogant, he was thrown down from his throne and deprived of his grandeur. He was cut off from human society and his heart became like that of a beast. He lived with wild asses and ate grass like an ox. He bathed with the dew of heaven until he learned the Most High God is ruler of all kingdoms and grants kingdoms to whomever the Most High wills.

Daniel castigated Belshazzar for not being more humble, despite his knowledge of all that happened to Nebuchadnezzar. He chastises Belshazzar for revolting against the Lord by bringing in the vessels of the Temple for his nobles, consorts, and concubines to drink wine from while praising the gods of silver and gold, bronze and iron, and wood and stone that see not, hear not, and lack intelligence. He reminds Belshazzar he refused to glorify the God whose hand is his very breath and the whole course of his life. The hand and the writing were sent by this God.

Daniel reads the words on the wall: MENE, TEKEL, and PERES. He explained that MENE meant God numbered Belshazzar's kingdom and put an end to it. TEKEL meant the king was weighed on the scales and found wanting. PERES meant the kingdom shall be divided and given to the Medes and Persians. The author of Daniel does not tell us about the reaction of Belshazzar at this news. Despite the bad news, Belshazzar ordered the servants to clothe Daniel in purple, put a gold chain around his neck, and proclaim him third in governing the kingdom. Belshazzar, the Chaldean king, was killed that same night.

Lectio Divina

Spend 8 to 10 minutes in silent contemplation of the following passage:

Whenever people make a decision that cannot be changed, they often remark: "The handwriting is on the wall!" The Book of Daniel, as we can see, is the source of this expression. The Lord has seen Belshazzar's hardness of heart and refusal to change, so the handwriting is on the wall. The unrepentant Belshazzar will pay for his sins. In this chapter, the Lord is giving all of us a message about the decisiveness of God. Jesus, speaking about pride and humility, said, "Rather, whoever wishes to be great among you will be your servant; whoever wishes to be first among you will be the slave of all" (Mark 10:43–44). The handwriting is on the wall!

✠ *What can I learn from this passage?*

Day 4: The Lions' Den (6)

King Darius the Mede appointed over his entire kingdom 120 satraps, that is, governors of provinces during the time of the Median and Persian empires. Although history accounts for three Persian kings named Darius, it does not name any King Darius for the Medes, who is named only in the Book of Daniel. Actually, the Median kingdom did not exist at the time treated in the Book of Daniel, since Cyrus of Persia had already conquered it.

The satraps chosen by Darius the Mede were accountable to three ministers, among whom was Daniel. The satraps reported to these ministers in order that the king would suffer no loss. Because Daniel possessed an exceptional spirit, leading him to surpass all the other ministers and satraps, the king considered placing him over the entire kingdom. The story of Daniel recalls that of Joseph, whom the Pharaoh made second in rank only to the Pharaoh himself. Joseph, like Daniel, was endowed with an exceptional spirit (see Genesis 41:37–46).

The other ministers and satraps continually searched for accusations they could make against Daniel regarding the kingdom, but they could find none, since Daniel was reliable without fault or corruption. The only fault they could find was not political, but religious. The ministers and satraps, knowing Daniel's reliance on the God of the Israelites, contrived a plot against him, convincing Darius to decree a thirty-day prohibition against making a petition to anyone, human or divine, except to the king. Without thinking of the consequences of such a prohibition, Darius signed it into law.

Although Daniel heard this law had been signed, he would go home to kneel in prayer and offer thanks to God three times daily in his upper chamber with the windows open toward Jerusalem. On one occasion, the ministers and satraps barged in and found Daniel praying and pleading before his God. They returned to the king, reminding him about the decree he signed against petitioning anyone, human or divine, except the king, for thirty days. The king's signature made it absolute and irreversible under the law of the Medes and the Persians. They then reported that

Daniel, one of the Jewish exiles, ignored the king and his decree by offering prayers three times a day. When the author was writing the Book of Daniel in the second century before Christ, he was acutely aware that King Antiochus IV was attempting to force the Jews into worshiping the Greek gods and not their own God.

When the king learned Daniel had disobeyed the decree, he became extremely distressed. He worked until sunset, attempting to find ways to rescue Daniel. Daniel's accusers pressured the king, reminding him that under the law of the Medes and the Persians, every royal prohibition or decree is irreversible. The king had no choice but to give the order for Daniel to be brought and cast into the lions' den. He told Daniel the God whom he served must be the one to save him now. The lions' den was a deep pit with walls too steep for anyone to scale. To avoid any tampering with the large stone blocking the opening to the den, the king sealed it with his own ring and the rings of the nobles after the stone was moved into place.

The king returned to his palace for the night, refusing to eat or be entertained. Finding sleep impossible, he rose very early the next morning and rushed to the lions' den. As he drew near, he cried out to Daniel in sorrow, calling him a servant of the living God whom he served so unwaveringly, and asking whether his God could save him from the lions. Darius apparently doubted Daniel would be saved, but he still hoped to find him alive. Daniel answered the king from the den, saying God sent an angel and closed the lions' mouths so they could not hurt him. Daniel declared he was found blameless before God and Darius.

The king reacted with joy and ordered Daniel to be brought up from the den. Because of his trust in the Lord, Daniel was brought up from the den unharmed. The king then ordered the men who had accused Daniel to be cast into the lions' den, along with their children and wives. Before they reached the bottom of the den, the lions pounced on them and crushed their bones.

Darius wrote to the nations and people of every language, decreeing the God of Daniel is to be revered and feared. His decree ended with a psalm praising Daniel's God as the living God, enduring forever, whose kingdom and sovereignty shall never end. He called the God of Daniel a savior and rescuer, who worked signs and wonders in heaven and on earth, and who saved Daniel from the lions' power. As a result, Daniel prospered during the reign of Darius and the reign of Cyrus the Persian.

Lectio Divina

Spend 8 to 10 minutes in silent contemplation of the following passage:

Daniel proved his love of the Lord by his willingness to remain faithful to the Lord, even in the face of death. There are Christians in countries today where they are being tortured or killed for their faith in God, yet they remain faithful to the Lord in the midst of their fear. These people are living in their own lions' den, and, like Daniel, are willing to die for the Lord. We must admire the faith and trust of these people and wonder how strong our faith would be in the midst of modern-day persecutions and killings.

✠ *What can I learn from this passage?*

Review Questions

1. What is the message of the fiery furnace?
2. How was Nebuchadnezzar's dream fulfilled?
3. What is the source of the saying, "The handwriting is on the wall?"
4. What is the message of Daniel in the lions' den?

The Book of Daniel (II)

DANIEL 7–14

Many of those who sleep in the dust of the earth shall awake; Some to everlasting life, others to reproach and everlasting disgrace (12:2).

Opening Prayer (SEE PAGE 15)

Context

Part 1: Daniel 7—8 Chapter 7 begins the apocalyptic visions of Daniel. The apocalyptic chapters were written and edited by different authors. Following the pattern of most apocalyptic writings, the authors of chapters 7 through 12 lived after the events described took place. They write as though they are living in a previous era, however, predicting the future.

Daniel had a vision of beasts that represented powerful nations that eventually met with destruction. One beast had ten horns, representing the succession of ten kings who caused a great deal of harm for the Israelites. He saw a small horn that represented King Antiochus IV, who persecuted the Jews and corrupted the Temple of the Lord. The battle of the great nations also appears in a battle between a he-goat and a two-horned ram that represented the kingdom of the Medes and Persians. The goat, representing the Greek army under Alexander the Great that came from the west, conquered the ram.

Part 2: Daniel 9—14 After two chapters describing the symbolic visions Daniel experienced, chapters 9—12 present revelations given to Daniel by an angel. The Lord decreed seventy weeks of years, which adds up to 490 years. At the end of this period, peace will be restored. The angel visits Daniel and warns him about the dangers ahead. One such threat the Jews of Judea must face will be Hellenism. The book presents one of the earliest writings concerning resurrection from the dead. The final chapters speak of the power of virtue over evil in the story of Susanna and the powerlessness of the false gods in the stories of the false god Bel and the false dragon god.

PART 1: GROUP STUDY (DANIEL 7—8)

Read aloud Daniel 7—8.

7 The Beasts and the Judgment

Daniel's apocalyptic vision begins in the first year of King Belshazzar of Babylon as Daniel had a dream that he (Daniel) wrote down. He saw the four winds of heaven suddenly stir up the great sea, out of which emerged four gigantic beasts, each one different from the others. These gigantic beasts refer to the nations symbolized in the dream of King Nebuchadnez-zar who saw a statue of gold, silver, iron, and clay in Daniel 2:36–45. The beasts represent the Babylonian, Median, Persian, and Greek kingdoms, which were the successive world kingdoms. The image of a beast is found in the apocalyptic writings of the Book of Revelation, where it refers to the Roman Empire. Daniel sees in his dream the four winds of the earth, which symbolize the winds coming from every direction, stirring up the great sea. People of ancient times believed that below the earth was a great sea where monsters dwelt.

Daniel saw four massive beasts emerge from the great sea. The first beast appeared to be a lion with eagle's wings. In ancient times, the kingdom of Babylon was often depicted as a lion with wings. While Daniel watched it, the wings were plucked. The plucking of the wings symbolized the loss of the kingdom. The plucking may refer to King Nebuchadnezzar and King

Belshazzar. The beast was "raised from the ground to stand on two feet like a human being, and given a human mind" (7:4). The human mind could refer to Nebuchadnezzar's release from insanity.

The second beast looked like a bear raised up on one side and having three tusks among the teeth in its mouth. It received the order to rise and devour much flesh. The bear symbolized the Median kingdom, and its tusks among the teeth symbolized the destructive power of the Medes who demolished their enemies.

Daniel then saw another beast, like a leopard, and on its back were four wings like those of a bird. It had four heads. Dominion was given to this beast. The leopard symbolized Persia, which moved swiftly in establishing its kingdom. Its four heads referred to the four Persian kings.

Daniel then saw a fourth beast, terrifying, horrible, and extremely strong. It had huge iron teeth with which it devoured and flattened nations and trampled what was left. Since elephants were used in war, the trampling could refer to elephants trampling down the earth. The fourth beast differed from the beasts that preceded it. The fourth beast was a reference to the most powerful kingdom of all, the Greek kingdom under Alexander.

After the death of Alexander in 323 BC, his generals fought for a portion of his kingdom, which was eventually split up among them. One portion was taken over by Seleucus I, who established the Seleucid dynasty. The fourth beast had ten horns, which represented the ten kings of the Seleucid dynasty who had the greatest effect on the Israelites. Daniel was considering the ten horns when a little horn came out of their midst. Three of the horns were pulled out to give it room. The eyes of this little horn were like human eyes, and it had a mouth that spoke with arrogance. The little horn is a reference to King Antiochus IV Epiphanes (175–164 BC), who usurped the throne from three of the Seleucid kings and persecuted the Jews.

As Daniel watched, thrones were set up, and God—the Ancient of Days—took his throne, wearing clothing as white as snow and having hair as pure as wool. This image resulted in later depictions of God as an old man, but the Ancient of Days actually refers to the one who always existed. It has nothing to do with age.

The Ancient of Days' throne consisted of flames of fire, complete with wheels of burning fire. A river of fire flowed out from where he sat, with thousands upon thousands ministering to him and multitudes upon multitudes attending to him.

As the court was convened, the books were opened. The court is the heavenly court, and the books represent the books detailing the deeds of humanity. Daniel watched from the time of the first of the arrogant words spoken by the horn until the beast was slain, its body destroyed and thrown into the fire. The dominion of the other beasts was removed, but they were given a continuation of their life for a time and a season. These other beasts were not destroyed as the fourth beast was.

As the visions continued, Daniel saw "coming with the clouds of heaven one like a son of man" (7:13). This reference has several different meanings in the Bible. Here, it refers to one who looked like a human being and who appears to be the archangel Michael. The son of man stands in contrast to the odious image of the beasts. When the one like the son of man reached the Ancient of Days and was brought before him, "He received dominion, splendor, and kingship; all nations, peoples and tongues will serve him" (7:14). In the Gospels, Jesus uses the term "Son of Man" to refer to himself. His dominion is everlasting. It will not pass away. And his kingship will not be destroyed.

Daniel reported his spirit was in anguish and terrified by the visions, a typical reaction to revelations in the Scriptures. He approached one of those present and asked the meaning of the vision. In previous chapters of Daniel, Daniel was the one who explains the visions, but in the apocalyptic visions, he needs the help of another to explain them to him. He learns the four beasts stand for the four kings who arise from the earth, but the holy ones of the Most High shall receive kingship and possess it forever.

Daniel wanted to know more about the four beasts, the ten horns, and the other horn. As he watched, the other horn attacked the holy ones and was victorious until the Ancient of Days arrived and pronounced judgment in favor of the holy ones of the Most High. The holy ones appear to refer to the Israelites. The time arrived for the holy ones to possess the kingship.

The one who explained the vision to Daniel explained the fourth beast, different from the others, would devour the whole earth and trample down and crush it. The ten horns refer to the ten kings of that kingdom. Another will rise up after them (Antiochus IV), who shall defeat three kings. He will speak against the Most High and wear down the holy ones, attempting to change the feast days and the law. This refers to the persecution of Antiochus IV, who desecrated the Temple. The Israelites will be in his power "for a time, two times, and half a time" (7:25), an apparent apocalyptic reference to three and a half years. Since seven is the perfect number, three and a half is half of seven, which makes it a number connoting evil.

When the heavenly court is convened and Antiochus' kingdom is abolished and destroyed, then the kingship, dominion, and majesty of all nations will come under the people of the holy ones of the Most High, that is, the Israelites. Their kingship shall last forever and all kingdoms shall serve and obey it.

Daniel declared this to be the end of his report. He was terrified and his face became pale, but he kept the matter to himself. This ends the section of the book written originally in Aramaic.

8 The Ram and the He-goat

Daniel had another vision in the third year of King Belshazzar in which he saw himself in the fortress of Susa in the province of Elam. Susa in the province of Elam is a reference to the royal palace of the kings of Persia. Daniel, who was beside the river Ulai, saw standing by the river a ram with two huge horns (Media and Persia), one larger and newer than the other. The ram was butting toward the west, north, and south, meaning the ram came out of the east. It grew so powerful that no beast could withstand it or be saved from its power.

As Daniel was reflecting, a he-goat with a prominent horn on its forehead appeared suddenly from the west, coming over the earth and never touching the ground. It rushed at the two-horned ram with a brutal and angry force, destroying both its horns. The ram lacked the power to withstand the he-goat, which heaved the ram to the ground and trampled on it. No one was able to rescue the ram. The he-goat appears to be the powerful army of Alexander the Great, which moved swiftly and aggressively across the land.

The he-goat (Alexander's army) grew very powerful, but at the height of its power, the great horn was shattered and was replaced by four other horns facing the four winds (north, south, east, and west). The great horn was Alexander himself, who died young and, after his death, his four generals divided his kingdom among them (the four horns). Out of one of the four horns came a little horn, which grew and covered the land toward the south, the east, and the glorious land (Jerusalem). It casts down to the earth the hosts of heaven and the stars and trampled on them. This symbolizes a cosmic disaster, where even the holy ones are trampled down. It grew even to the prince of the host, the Most High God, removing the daily sacrifice made in the Temple and desecrating the sanctuary of the Lord. It cast the truth (true worship) to the ground and succeeded in all it did.

In his vision, Daniel heard the holy ones speaking, asking how long the events concerning the daily sacrifice, the desolating sin, and the defiling of the sanctuary would continue. The desolating sin appears to be a reference to the placing of a statue of the pagan god Zeus in the Temple or the placing of some other pagan altar. The answer was that it shall continue for 2,300 evenings and mornings. By saying evenings and mornings, the speaker is alluding to the times for sacrifice. After that time, the sanctuary shall be restored to its true state.

When Daniel sought the meaning of the vision, one who looked like a man stood before him, and he heard a human voice cry out, "Gabriel, explain the vision to this man." When Gabriel (the one who looked like a man) approached him, Daniel fell in terror, and Gabriel told him the vision refers to the end time. Daniel fell forward, unconscious, but Gabriel touched him and made him stand up. Gabriel informed Daniel he will learn what will happen in the "last days of wrath," the day for judgment.

Gabriel explained the two-horned ram Daniel saw represents the kings of the Medes and Persians, and the he-goat represents the king of the Greeks; the huge horn on its forehead is the first king of the Greeks, the four horns that rose in its place were the four kingdoms issuing from this kingdom but lacking its strength.

When their reign ends and sinners have reached their limit, a disrespectful and powerful king, skilled in intrigue, will cause terrifying ruin and succeed in his endeavors. He shall annihilate mighty people, his deceptiveness shall be turned against the holy ones (the people), and he will succeed. He shall be proud and destroy many by his deceptiveness. When, however, he challenges the prince of princes (God) he shall be defeated without a hand being raised. Antiochus IV died in battle in 164

BC. Gabriel told Daniel his visions were true, and he must keep this vision secret because it reveals the distant future.

Daniel was weak and sick for several days, but he arose and took care of the king's business. The vision, however, left him confused, without understanding.

Review Questions

1. What is the meaning of the symbol of the four beasts?
2. What is the meaning of the symbol of the ten horns?
3. What is the little horn and why is it important?

Closing Prayer (SEE PAGE 15)

Pray the closing prayer now or after *lectio divina*.

Lectio Divina (SEE PAGE 8)

Relax your body and maintain a posture of prayer (back straight, eyes shut, feet flat on the floor). This exercise can take as long as you want, but in the context of this Bible study, 10 to 20 minutes should be sufficient.

The meditations that follow are provided only to help group participants use this prayer form, but note that *lectio* is intended to bring one to a place of prayerful contemplation where the Word of God speaks to the hearer from his or her heart. (See page 8 for further instruction.)

The Beasts and the Judgment (7)

When we read about the four beasts and the eventual destruction of their kingdoms, we may ask why God waited so long to help the people. For those alive at the time when the Jews were freed from Babylon, it was a great day, but before that day, many suffered and died unmercifully. In our own day, we read about soldiers who gave their lives so others may be free. It seems so many must die for others to enjoy the fruits of their death. Life is indeed a mystery, but it also challenges us to ask ourselves what we do with the freedom that cost the lives of so many.

✠ *What can I learn from this passage?*

The Ram and the He-goat (8)

The desire to be stronger or richer drove many ancient countries to battle with each other. Kingdom after kingdom sought to conquer more lands to feed their pride, and, in the end, other, stronger countries conquered them. Their pride led to their downfall. In the world today, some people hurt others for the sake of their own gain, even though they have more than enough to satisfy their needs. The healthiest and happiest people of the world seem to be those who work honestly and are content with the gifts God gave them without striving to be richer or better off than their neighbors.

✠ *What can I learn from this passage?*

PART 2: INDIVIDUAL STUDY (DANIEL 9—14)

Day 1: Seventy Weeks of Years (9)

Daniel begins by dating the following events in the first year of Darius the Mede. Since nowhere else is Darius the Mede found except in the Book of Daniel, his father's name, Ahasuerus, is also most likely fictitious. The date means nothing to the reader, and the chronological order of the events in the chapter is not accurate. Daniel speaks of finding in the books a decree of the Lord to the prophet Jeremiah that Jerusalem would remain in ruins for seventy years (see Jeremiah 25:11–12 and 29:10). The "books" refer to the Scriptures, and this sort of citation is rarely found from the biblical writers of the Old Testament. Daniel wonders why Jeremiah's prediction of restoration after seventy years was not fulfilled. For an answer, Daniel prays to the Lord God in prayer and petition, with fasting, sackcloth, and ashes, all signs of mourning.

The prayer in Daniel 9:4–19 is a later addition to the book. In the prayer, Daniel addresses the Lord as a great and awesome God who keeps the covenant and who shows mercy to those who love the Lord and follow the Lord's commandments and precepts. The prayer is not a prayer of an individual but of a community. They have sinned, rebelling against the Lord's commandments and precepts. They have not obeyed the Lord's servants, the prophets, who spoke in the name of the Lord to their kings, princes, ancestors, and all the Israelites.

Justice is on the side of the Lord, while the people of Judah, Jerusalem, and all Israel—who were scattered near and far—live in shame because of their betrayal of the Lord. They acknowledge their sins and shame, like the shame of their kings, princes, and ancestors. Despite their refusal to listen to the voice of the Lord calling them through the prophets to walk according to the laws of the Lord, they also realize the Lord is compassionate and forgiving. The curse and oath in the Law of Moses affected them because the Israelites sinned, refusing to listen to the Lord (see Deuteronomy 28:15–45).

The Lord fulfilled the words of Deuteronomy by bringing disaster upon them and their rulers, a devastation never seen before as that of Jerusalem. As it is written in the law of the Lord, the curse of the Lord will bring affliction (see Leviticus 26:14–16 and Deuteronomy 28:15–17). This is the first time the expression "as it is written" is used in the Bible. The community recognizes the Lord is just in all the Lord does, and the devastation came upon them because they refused to listen to the voice of the Lord.

The prayer recognizes the power of the Lord in leading their ancestors out of Egypt, which made the name of the Lord known among the nations, and prays the Lord's anger will be turned away from Jerusalem, which is the Lord's holy mountain. The people admit, because of the sins of the Israelites and their ancestors, Jerusalem and the Lord's people have become a scandal among all their neighbors. They pray the Lord will hear their prayer for the Lord's own sake and that the face of the Lord will shed light upon the Lord's desolate sanctuary.

Recognizing their sinfulness, the people beg the Lord to look upon the anguish of the city where the people invoke the name of the Lord and ask for mercy. They beg the Lord to hear and be attentive to their prayer, acting without delay for the sake of the Lord whose name the city and people bear. Daniel continued praying, confessing his sin and the sin of the people, and petitioning the Lord concerning Jerusalem, the holy mountain of God. At this point, the prayer inserted in this portion of the text ends.

The prayer inserted by a different author from verses 4 to 19 ends here, and the chapter returns to Daniel's quest for an answer to his question concerning Jeremiah's prophecy saying the land of Jerusalem would lay in ruin for seventy years. Gabriel, whom Daniel had seen in an earlier vision, came to him in flight at the time of the evening offering. The image of the angel's flight stresses the swiftness of an angelic visit. The evening offering took place between 3 and 4 in the afternoon. Gabriel informs Daniel, because he is beloved by the Lord, he came to give him understanding in answer to his prayer.

The angel states the Lord has decreed "seventy weeks" for the Israelites and the holy city. This time frame, of course, is symbolic instead of literal, and was understood to mean seven times seventy years, or 490 years. Each time the apocalyptic vision tells the number of weeks, the weeks are interpreted to mean years and are multiplied by seven. The 490 years refer to the period between Jeremiah's statement and the death of Antiochus IV. Since this is apocalyptic writing, the reckoning of the number of years for each part of the prophecy will not follow the actual historical number of years. For apocalyptic writers, the symbolism is more important than exact dating.

At the end of seventy weeks of seventy years, when Jerusalem is again free from the grip of Antiochus IV, the transgressions and evil of the people will end, their guilt will be cleansed, unending justice will commence, visions and prophecies fulfilled, and the holy of holies anointed.

From the time of Jeremiah's prediction until an anointed ruler arises, there shall be seven weeks. Seven weeks multiplied by seven years are forty-nine years, about the time of the exile. The anointed ruler could refer to Cyrus, the Persian king who allowed the Israelites to return to their homeland, or to the high priest Jeshua, who presided over the rebuilding of the altar of sacrifice after the exile (see Ezra 3:2).

The holy city will be rebuilt in sixty-two weeks. Seven times sixty-two is 434 years, about the period between the rebuilding of Jerusalem after the exile and the beginning of the Seleucid persecution. At that time, an anointed one will be cut down with no one to help him. This refers to Onias III, the deposed high priest of Israel, who was murdered in 171 BC. The people of a leader (Antiochus IV Epiphanes) will come and destroy the city and the sanctuary. He shall come like a flood until the end of the war, a reference to the overwhelming onslaught and the destruction of the city and Temple.

For one week (seven years), Antiochus shall make a firm covenant with many of the upper class, a reference to the Jews who wanted to retain the Hellenistic and pagan way of life. For half a week (three and a half years), he shall do away with sacrifice and offering. Desolation of the land and the abomination of the Temple will take place until the Temple is totally destroyed.

Although the numbers in the text add up to 490 years, the actual years counting from Jeremiah's prophecy to the end of the reign of Antiochus IV would be 441 years.

Lectio Divina

Spend 8 to 10 minutes in silent contemplation of the following passage:

Life is a mystery. Why are some people born in a land of freedom where they have opportunities to fulfill their life's goals while others are born in war-torn areas where there are no schools and where the terror of whistling rockets is heard every day? Why are some born in appalling poverty while others live a comfortable and secure life? Why are some born into loving families and others born into broken families? The list can go on. The books of the prophets say punishment comes to the people because they turn their backs on God, but we read about evil people who are prospering financially. Our call in life is to develop the gifts God has given to us and to use them wisely. If we are blessed, then bring that blessing to others.

✠ *What can I learn from this passage?*

Day 2: An Angelic Vision (10)

Daniel receives a revelation in the third year of Cyrus, king of Persia, which would be 536 BC. The author of the book identifies Daniel by his Babylonian name, which we already learned is Belteshazzar. The revelation Daniel received in a vision concerned a great war, which commentators are not able to identify due to the uncertainty of the original expression in the Hebrew text, which could be translated in several different ways.

Daniel mourned for three weeks, consuming no rich food, meat or wine, and not anointing himself until the three weeks ended. The mourning and fasting does not seem to be a result of the vision, but a preparation for the visions ahead.

Daniel tells us, on the twenty-fourth day of the first month he was on the bank of the great Tigris River where he saw a man dressed in linen with a belt of fine gold around his waist. The man appears to be the angel Gabriel. The man's body shone like crystal gems, his face like lightning, his eyes like fiery torches, his arms and feet like polished bronze, and the sound of his voice like the roar of a large crowd. Daniel alone witnessed the vision, but those with him fled in fear and hid themselves, even though they did not see the vision. Daniel became weak and powerless and his face became as pale as death. When Daniel heard the man's voice, he fell face forward, unconscious.

A hand touched Daniel, raising him to his hands and knees. The man, addressing Daniel as beloved, directed him to understand the words he was speaking to him. Daniel stood and the man told him not to fear. Often, when angels appear, their immediate words inform the recipient of the vision to have no fear. The man told Daniel, from the first day he sought wisdom and humbled himself before God, the Lord heard his prayer.

The man explained why it took so long for him to come to Daniel. He said the prince of the kingdom of Persia stood in his way for twenty-one days, until Michael, one of the chief princes, came to help him. Michael is the patron angel of Israel. In ancient Judaism, the people believed each nation had a patron protecting it. The prince of the kingdom of Persia refers to the patron angel of Persia. In the Book of Sirach, we learn the Lord set a ruler over every nation, which is really a reference to a patron (see Sirach 17:17). The man left Michael with the king of Persia and came to Daniel to help him understand what shall happen to the people in the last days, for a vision is yet to come about those days. Apocalyptic writings often speak of the last days.

While the man was speaking, Daniel fell face forward and kept silent, apparently in some form of trance. Something like a hand touched his lips and he informed the one standing before him that he was overcome with fear at the vision. He became so weak he asked how he, the lord's servant, could speak with his lord. In using "lord" in this context, Daniel is not referring to God, but to the man speaking to him. The man calmed Daniel, telling him not to fear, but to be peaceful, courageous, and strong.

When the man spoke, Daniel became strong and told the man to speak. The man informed Daniel he (the man) must soon fight the prince of Persia again and speaks of the arrival of the prince of Greece. The prince of Greece could refer to Alexander or to Antiochus IV. Since the purpose of the man's visit is to bring understanding to Daniel, Daniel will learn from the man what is written in the book of truth. The book of truth is a heavenly book in which future events are already written.

The man explains no one supports him (the man) against these enemies of the princes of Persia and Greece except Michael, who is a prince to Daniel. The man refers back to the first year of Darius the Mede, saying he strengthened Darius and was his refuge. The link with the first year of Darius the Mede recalls the events which took place in that first year as expressed in chapter 9. In chapter 9, the man who visited Daniel is identified as Gabriel (see 9:21).

Lectio Divina

Spend 8 to 10 minutes in silent contemplation of the following passage:

Gabriel appeared to Daniel as a powerful and brilliantly shining human being. Daniel does not immediately realize he is speaking to an angel, but he gradually learns the identity of the man, and he himself grows stronger. The Lord often sends angels into our life, not spiritual angels but angels who are ordinary men and women like ourselves who inspire, encourage, and challenge us. We all have talents and need angels to inspire us to use our talents to their fullest for the good of others. The man, who was the angel Gabriel, gave strength to Daniel in the same way *we* gain strength from the encouragement of angels in our life.

✠ *What can I learn from this passage?*

Day 3: The Hellenistic Age (11—12)

Daniel received word about the fall of Persia, the rise of the Greek Empire under Alexander the Great, and the division of the Greek Empire after Alexander's death. Since the author acts as though he were writing at the time the Israelites returned from exile, he speaks as though he was alive while Cyrus was the first king of Persia. The author speaks of Gabriel as the one who predicts future events. In the vision, Gabriel foresees three more kings of Persia, with the fourth one being the richest of all who will battle against the Greeks. The idea of the fourth being the richest is doubtful. There were actually more than four kings of Persia, but the Jews of second century BC, when the Book of Daniel was being written, knew of only four.

Gabriel predicted "a powerful king" (11:3) will arise and rule with great power, but within a short period of time, his kingdom shall be broken and split in four directions under heaven. "The powerful king" refers to Alexander the Great, who conquered the Persian Empire in 333 BC and died young. His kingdom was not divided among his descendants, but it later broke into four smaller kingdoms, ruled by his generals. The author of Daniel tells us the kingdom will be torn apart and ruled by others.

Although the kingdom was divided into four, the Jewish concern centered on the two divisions causing havoc for the Jews, the kingdoms to the north (Syria) and south (Egypt) of Palestine. Chapters 11 and 12 describe the events taking place under the rule of these two kingdoms, with the greatest threat coming from the northern kingdom. Gabriel predicted the king of the south will grow strong. This king was Ptolemy I (323–285 BC), who founded the kingdom of the Ptolemies in Egypt. Gabriel predicted one of Ptolemy's princes would grow stronger and govern a domain greater than that of Ptolemy I.

King Seleucus I (312–280 BC) became the ruler of the Seleucid kingdom north of Palestine. In 252, Ptolemy II and Antiochus II of the Seleucid kingdom established an alliance when Ptolemy II gave his daughter, Berenice, in marriage to Antiochus II, who divorced his previous wife. Instead of giving the right of succession to the child of his previous wife, he gave the right to succession to Berenice's child. Gabriel predicted Berenice, her offspring, and those who came with her would not survive.

Antiochus divorced Berenice and took back his previous wife. His remarried wife took advantage of the situation and was able to have Antiochus II, Berenice, their infant son, and her Egyptian entourage killed. In revenge, Ptolemy III, the brother of Berenice, invaded the land of the Seleucids (Syria), defeated Seleucus II, and carried off plunder, including images of their gods and their precious metals of silver and gold to Egypt.

Gabriel predicted the king of the north would invade the land of the king of the south. Seleucus II set up a counterattack against Ptolemy III, who was forced to return home to Egypt. Gabriel predicted the sons of Seleucus II would attack Egypt like a flood surging around its stronghold. The king of the south (Egypt) then engaged the large army of the Seleucids in battle and defeated them. Gabriel predicted the king of the north would raise another large army and, after some years, attack and take the king of the south by storm. This battle in which the Seleucids defeated the Ptolemies took place in "the glorious land," namely Palestine, leaving the land under the power of the Seleucids.

In 194 BC, an alliance was established when Cleopatra, the daughter of Antiochus III, married Ptolemy V. Gabriel predicted Antiochus III would return to the coastland where he would be successful for a time, but a Roman consul would defeat and weaken him so badly he would be forced to return to his homeland. He was later killed and his successor, Seleucus IV, who controlled Palestine, sent a collector of tribute to seize the treasury of the Jerusalem Temple. He was later murdered, but not in battle.

Gabriel predicted a loathsome person shall become king in his place, namely Antiochus IV Epiphanes, who, not having the right to the royal insignia, usurped the kingship. Antiochus IV becomes the most hateful of the Seleucid rulers. Gabriel predicted he shall crush armed forces and kill the prince of the covenant, a reference to the Jewish high priest, Onias III, who was murdered at the court of Antiochus IV. He shall become more powerful through treachery, deception, and fraud. This prediction referred to the defeat of King Ptolemy VII of Egypt, who despite his strong army was betrayed by his friends and defeated by Antiochus IV. Gabriel predicted the two kings shall sit at table together and exchange lies. King Ptolemy VII and Antiochus IV gave the appearance of negotiating but were actually lying to each other.

Gabriel predicted Antioch IV shall return home with great riches. He managed another campaign but was forced by a Roman army (ships of the Kittim) to leave Egypt. Gabriel predicted he would rage against the holy covenant, which referred to his plundering of the Temple and his action of favoring those who abandoned the covenant. At his command, armed forces will rise and defile the sanctuary, doing away with the daily sacrifices and setting up the "desolating abomination," a statue of Zeus set up in the Temple.

Gabriel predicts Antiochus IV shall be successful in making some of the people disloyal to the covenant, but those with spiritual wisdom will instruct and protect the people. This could be a reference to the Maccabean revolt against Antiochus IV. A time of bloodshed, flames, exile, and plunder will cause the Jews to stumble, but they will be helped. Some of those who remain faithful will stumble (struggle) so that they may be tested, refined, and purified until the appointed end time.

Gabriel predicted King Antiochus IV shall do what he wills, making himself greater than any god while blaspheming the God of gods, the Lord of Israel. He shall prosper until the wrath of God has reached its end. What is decided must happen. Because Antiochus IV shall consider himself greater than all, he shall have no regard for other gods. Instead, he shall glorify only the god of strongholds. This is a reference to the god worshiped in a fortress he established in Jerusalem. He shall glorify a god unknown to his ancestors with gold, silver, precious stones, and similar expensive gifts. He shall act in favor of those who build up the strongholds, the people who worship a foreign god. He shall bestow great honor on them, placing them as rulers over many people and shall distribute the land as a reward for those who worship as he desires.

The images presented in Gabriel's prediction did not take place. The king of the south will challenge Antiochus IV, but Antiochus shall overwhelm them with his chariots, horsemen, and powerful army, surging through the land like a great flood. He shall invade the magnificent land where many will fall, with the exception of Edom, Moab, and a major portion of Ammon, all of whom will escape his control. His power over the land shall be so extensive that even Egypt will not escape his wrath. He shall possess the gold, silver, and all the treasures of Egypt. Libya and Ethiopia shall be in his entourage. When he shall receive bad news from the east and the north, he shall march in anger to obliterate them, putting them under the ban. He shall pitch his tent between the seas and the royal holy mountain. When he reaches his end, no one will help him.

Chapter 12 gives the first clear reference to resurrection from the dead, final judgment, and afterlife found in the Bible. Michael, the great prince and patron of Israel, shall rise. Typical of apocalyptic writings, the description of the end time is described as one unsurpassed. Everyone found written in the book of life will escape. Many sleeping in the dust of the earth will awake, which means the dead will rise. In using the word "many," this passage seems to indicate not all will rise. Some will rise to everlasting life and others to reproach and everlasting disgrace. The wise will shine brilliantly like the majesty of the firmament and those who lead many to justice will be like the stars forever.

Typical of apocalyptic visions, the message is to be kept secret and the book sealed until the end of time. In the meanwhile, many shall roam aimlessly and wickedness shall increase.

Daniel saw two angels, one on either bank of the river. One asked the man who was upstream and clothed in linen how long it would be before these dreadful things would happen. The man lifted his hands to heaven and Daniel heard him swear by the one who lives forever that it should be for a time, two times, and half a time, which means three and a half years, when the power of the destroyer of the holy people would be brought to an end, then all these things should end. Daniel, who heard but did not understand, asked what follows this. He received the message that the words are to be kept secret and sealed until the end time. During that time, many shall be refined, purified, and tested, and the wicked shall be proven wicked; the wicked shall not understand, but those with the angels shall.

The man declared, from the time the daily sacrifice is abolished and the desolating abomination is set up, there shall be 1,290 days. This refers to the period when the Temple is desecrated and the people are unable to offer sacrifices. Those who show patience and perseverance in these days will be blessed. The man tells Daniel to take his rest and promises he shall rise for his reward at the end of days. Daniel will share in this resurrection.

Lectio Divina

Spend 8 to 10 minutes in silent contemplation of the following passage:

> The history of the world depicts many periods when believers had to suffer for their faith. In Daniel's era, the people suffered, not in exile, but in their own country. A little less than two centuries before Christ, a faithful Jew could expect death if he or she disobeyed the law of Antiochus IV, who defiled the Temple and forbad the people to worship their God. Today in many countries, Christian churches are being defiled and destroyed, and those who proclaim themselves to be Christian are still being martyred for their faith.

✠ *What can I learn from this passage?*

Day 4: Susanna (13)

The story of Susanna reads like a parable. A man named Joakim married Susanna, who is described as very beautiful and God-fearing. Her parents were blameless in the eyes of the Lord and trained their daughter to follow the Law of Moses. Joakim, who was very rich, had a garden near his home.

The author relates that two elders were appointed as judges that year. It is unclear what "that year" is. The Lord commented on their appointment by saying wickedness has come out of Babylon, referring to the wickedness of the elders chosen to govern the people.

The judges often visited the house of Joakim and, after all the other people departed, they would see Susanna enter the garden every day around noon. Two judges lusted after Susanna. The two elders would not allow their eyes look toward heaven (God), a sign they had abandoned faith in the Lord and worshiped the gods of Babylon.

Because the two judges were ashamed to tell each other about lusting after Susanna, they kept their desires to themselves. One day, they both acted as though they were going home for their noon meal, but soon after they left, they turned back and arrived at the same spot. When they questioned each other concerning their return, they both had to admit their lust for Susanna and agreed to seek an opportunity when they would find her alone.

One day, Susanna entered the garden with two maids. Unaware that the two elders had hidden themselves in the garden and were watching her, she ordered her maids to bring her oil and soap and to close the gates while she bathed. The order to close the gates stresses the modesty of Susanna. The maids, not knowing the judges were present, did as she ordered, leaving to get the supplies she wanted. They shut the gates as they left.

When the maids left, the two old men came out of hiding and ran to her. Noting the garden doors were shut and no one could see them, they declared they wanted her and threatened to testify against her if she refused their advances. They would testify a young man was with her, which, they would claim, was the reason she sent away her two maids.

Susanna, as a faithful Jew, knew she was trapped, saying it would mean death for her if she complied, since adultery was punishable by death, or she would be in the power of the judges if she refused. She declared she would rather be in their power than sin against the Lord. She screamed and the two old men shouted with her, as one of them ran and opened the gates to the garden. According to the Law of Moses, a woman about to be raped must scream out loud or receive the same fate as a woman who commits adultery, which is death (see Deuteronomy 22:24).

When the people in the house heard the screams, they ran in by the side gate to see what was happening to her. Immediately, the old men accused her of being with a young man. Since the sin of the wife of the master of a household would bring shame upon the whole household, the servants felt shame for her. The author states nothing like this had ever been said before about Susanna, implying she was already considered guilty despite her untarnished reputation.

The next day, along with the people, the two wicked old men came to Joakim, Susanna's husband, to testify against her with the evil intention of condemning her to death. They sent for Susanna and she came with her parents, children, and all her relatives, who, according to custom, would also be sharing in her shame. She was elegant and beautiful. As her modesty demanded, her face was veiled, but the two transgressors of the law ordered the veil removed so they could satisfy themselves with her beauty revealed. To stand unveiled before all the people would bring shame upon her and her relatives. Everyone was weeping.

In front of the people, the two old men laid their hands on her head, a symbolic act used by a person's accusers. According to Deuteronomy 19:15, the testimony of at least two witnesses is needed. Susanna wept as she looked up to heaven, fully trusting the Lord.

The two men testified they were walking in the garden when Susanna entered with two maids, shut the garden gates, and sent the maids away. They then witnessed a young man, who was hidden in the garden, come and lie with her. When the men saw this evil act, they ran toward them lying together and tried to capture the young man, but he, being too strong for them, opened the gates and escaped. They seized Susanna and asked her to identify the young man, but she refused. The two men testified to the truth of their statement.

Since the two men were elders and judges of the people, the assembly believed their story and condemned Susanna to death. Susanna, however, prayed aloud to the eternal God, whom she declared knows what is hidden, knows all things before they occur, and knows these men testified falsely. She proclaimed she was about to die, although she was innocent. In accord with the Law of Moses, she realized the Lord is the true judge (see Deuteronomy 19:16–21).

The Lord heard her prayer and stirred up the holy spirit of a young boy named Daniel, who shouted out he was innocent of this woman's blood. Prophets were often stirred up by the spirit to prophesy with wisdom. The author is not alluding to the Holy Spirit as explained in the New Testament.

When someone was condemned by the community, the responsibility for the judgment falls on the community. Accepting a false judgment would make everyone guilty. Recognizing their responsibility, the people inquired about what he was saying. Daniel asked the Israelites if they were so foolish as to condemn a daughter of Israel without investigation and clear evidence. He ordered the people to return to court because the elders had testified falsely against her.

The people quickly returned to court, and the rest of the elders invited the young Daniel to sit with them, since God had given him the wisdom of old age. By speaking of the rest of the elders, the author was alluding to other elders in the group who were innocent. Daniel told them to separate the two men from each other for him to examine them.

After they were separated, Daniel had the first man brought in and accused him of having grown wicked with age. He stated the man's past sins will now come to term, saying the judge, despite the Lord's command that the innocent and just shall not be put to death, passed unjust sentences, condemned the innocent, and freed the guilty. He then asked the judge to tell everyone under which tree the judge caught Susanna and the young man. The judge replied, "Under a mastic tree." Daniel responded the judge's fine lie has cost him his head; an angel of God has already received the verdict from God and will split him in two.

Daniel then ordered the people to bring in the other elder. He addressed him as an offspring of Canaan, not of Judah, which would mean the judge had abandoned the Lord of the Israelites for the gods of the Canaanites. Daniel declared beauty had enticed him and lust had filled his heart. He accused him of acting wickedly with the daughters of Israel who followed his judgment because they feared him. In speaking of the daughters of Israel, the author of the parable is referring to the northern kingdom that was destroyed by the Assyrians in 721 BC. The people of the northern kingdom of Israel sinned against the Lord by worshiping idols.

Daniel then spoke of Susanna as a daughter of Judah. By using the term "daughter of Judah," the author is referring to the Jews after their return from exile in Babylon and implying Susanna is a faithful Jew. Daniel then asked the man to tell him under which tree they surprised the man and the woman together. The judge answered, "Under an oak." Daniel proclaimed that his fine lie cost him his head. He declared that an angel of God waits with a sword to cut the two in half and destroy both of them.

The assembly cried out, praising God. They then sentenced to death the two old men, whose own words condemned them. In accordance with the Law of Moses, the verdict of the same form of death planned for Susanna would be inflicted on the two elders (see Deuteronomy 19:16–21). The author writes that innocent blood was spared on that day. When the shame Susanna, Joakim, and all her relatives felt was removed, Susanna's parents praised God.

Lectio Divina

Spend 8 to 10 minutes in silent contemplation of the following passage:

> Joseph Cardinal Bernardin of Chicago was accused of sinning with an underage boy. When the accusation was later proven false, Cardinal Bernardin told how deeply painful it was to endure such an embarrassing and false accusation. Cardinal Bernardin, however, was not bound by the Law of Moses, but by the Law of Christ, and, instead of punishing his accuser, Cardinal Bernardin visited him and forgave him. False accusations still happen, but it seems real saints trust in God, as Susanna did.

✠ *What can I learn from this passage?*

Day 5: Bel and the Dragon (14)

This chapter contains three short stories about Daniel's encounter with those who worship false gods and the triumph of the one true God over the false gods of the Babylonians. The first story begins in 550 BC, after Cyrus, the Persian king, defeated King Astyages, the last king of the Medes. The author believed the Medes and Persians ruled Babylon and worshiped their gods after their destruction of Babylon. Commentators speculate the following story about Daniel was written sometime during the period of the Persian Empire (circa 539 to 333 BC) and was placed at the end of the Book of Daniel by a later editor.

In the story, Daniel was the highly honored friend of the king who, along with all the Babylonians, worshiped an idol called Bel. Every day, the Babylonians provided six bushels of the finest flour, forty sheep, and six measures of wine for Bel. When the king asked Daniel why he did not worship Bel, Daniel answered he did not worship idols, but only his God who made heaven and earth and has dominion over all living creatures.

The king challenged Daniel's disbelief, pointing out all the food the idol eats each day. Daniel laughed, telling the king not to be deceived by thinking an idol, which is clay on the inside and bronze on the outside, had eaten or drunk anything. The king sent for the priests and ordered them to tell him who consumed the provisions offered to Bel. If they were the ones who consumed the provisions, they would die, and if they proved Bel consumed them, then Daniel would die for blaspheming Bel. Daniel agreed with this arrangement.

There were seventy priests of Bel, in addition to their wives and children. When the king and Daniel went into the Temple of Bel, the priests left so the king could set out the food and prepare the wine in their absence. Preparing the wine involved mixing it with water and spices. The priests told the king to close the door of the Temple when he was finished and to seal it with the insignia on his ring. If the king finds the provisions remaining in the morning, then the priests acknowledge they will die, but if the provisions are consumed, then Daniel shall die. Since the priests had constructed a secret entrance under the table through which they entered to consume the food each day, the closed door did not concern them.

When the priests departed and the king set the food before Bel, Daniel ordered servants to scatter some ashes throughout the whole Temple. After the king sealed the door, he and Daniel left. That night, the priests entered the Temple with their wives and children, as they usually did, and ate and drank all the offerings.

The next morning, Daniel and the king arrived at the door of the Temple and agreed the seal on the door was unbroken. When they opened the door, the king saw the food and drink had disappeared, and he praised Bel. Daniel, laughing, held the king back from entering the Temple area. Pointing to the floor, he asked who made the footprints. The king recognized the footprints of men, women, and children. The king, apparently unaware of Daniel's plot of having servants scatter the ashes in the Temple, became enraged and arrested the priests, their wives, and children. When the priests revealed their secret entrance, the king had them put to death. He handed the idol, Bel, over to Daniel, who destroyed it and the Temple.

A second story tells of a great dragon worshiped by the Babylonians. In ancient times, a dragon often referred to a large snake. Since Daniel could not deny the dragon was a living god, the king ordered Daniel to worship it. The idea of the dragon being a living god contrasts with the dead idol of the first story and serves as a link with the first story. Replying he worshiped only his Lord and God who is the true living God, Daniel asked for permission to kill the dragon, promising to kill it without a sword or club.

The king gave permission. Daniel boiled some pitch, fat, and hair, which he made into cakes. He put them into the mouth of the dragon, who ate them and burst. Daniel showed the king what he was worshiping.

The people became angry, accusing the king of becoming a Jew because he destroyed Bel, killed the dragon, and put the priests to death. They demanded the king hand Daniel over to them or they would kill the king and his family. The king surrendered to the pressure of the people and turned Daniel over to them. They threw Daniel into the lions' den, where he remained for six days with seven lions. The story of Daniel in the lions' den recalls the story of Daniel in the lions' den found in chapter six of this book. In the story in chapter six, Daniel was in the lions' den for only one night. The author of the story in chapter 14 mentions the lions ordinarily received two carcasses and two sheep each day, but now they received nothing so they would surely devour Daniel.

A prophet named Habakkuk was in Judea. Habakkuk prophesied around 612–597 BC, long before the events described in this story, a fact which provides further evidence a later author constructed the story to convey a message concerning the power of the Lord and the powerlessness of the false gods. Habakkuk mixed some bread in a bowl with stew and was about to bring it to the reapers in the field when an angel of the Lord told him to bring the meal to Daniel in the lions' den. Habakkuk objected, saying he never went to Babylon and knew nothing about a den. The angel carried him by the hair of his head and set him down in Babylon above the lions' den. Habakkuk cried out to Daniel to take the meal God sent him. Daniel praised the Lord for remembering him. As Daniel ate, the angel carried Habakkuk back to his own place.

On the seventh day, the king came to the den to mourn Daniel, but he found him sitting in the den unharmed. The king cried out in a loud voice, praising the Lord and God of Daniel and proclaiming there was no other god except the God of Daniel. When he brought Daniel out of the den, he ordered those who accused him be cast into the den. In sight of the king, the lions instantly devoured them.

Lectio Divina

Spend 8 to 10 minutes in silent contemplation of the following passage:

In the homes of many Catholics, a person often finds statues and pictures representing Jesus, Mary, or some of the saints. Unlike the kings of Babylon who worshiped images of the gods, Catholics do not worship statues or pictures but use them as reminders of these holy people. Catholics realize that statues and pictures are no more than metal, plastic, or paper. Life is filled with many distractions, and there are times when we need an image or object to redirect our minds to God. Just as people place pictures of relatives in their homes to remind them of their loved ones, so Catholics do the same with statues and pictures of Jesus, Mary, and the saints. When used correctly, the practice of placing religious statues or pictures in our homes is a meaningful addition to our everyday environment and helps with our spiritual growth.

✠ *What can I learn from this passage?*

Review Questions

1. What is the significance of the seventy weeks of years?
2. What is the history of the Hellenistic Age?
3. Why is Daniel's message about resurrection so significant?
4. How do the incidents in the story of Susanna demonstrate the battle of good and evil?

CPSIA information can be obtained at www.ICGtesting.com
Printed in the USA
LVOW10s0555090414

380777LV00005B/5/P